Praise for

Leading with a Limp

"There are good books on leadership, but this one is profound. It is better than a 'how to do it' book; this is a 'how to *be* it' book for leaders. Dan Allender offers serious wisdom rather than simple platitudes."

—MARK SANBORN, speaker, leadership consultant, and best-selling
author of *The Fred Factor*

"Not only is Dan Allender a good friend, he is a great leader. In *Leading with a Limp,* he has shown us how we can effectively lead those allotted to our charge. Read this book; it will bring a lot of things into perspective for you."

—DENNIS RAINEY, president of FamilyLife and coauthor
of *Moments Together for Couples*

"After I read this book, the first two words out of my mouth were 'At last!' Amid a deluge of spiritual gifts' inventories, at last there is someone who understands how God's strength is made *perfect* in our imperfections. At last someone has brought spiritual strengths and spiritual weaknesses into conversation. For Dan Allender, the limp is a limpid way of walking that leads into the very presence of God."

—LEONARD SWEET, author of *The Three Hardest Words*
and *Out of the Question…Into the Mystery*

"*Leading with a Limp* is not your basic cafeteria-brand manual on how to do leadership. It is a call to openly face your shortcomings as a leader. Dan Allender reminds us that our greatest asset as leaders is not our competence but the courage to name and deal with our frailties and imperfections."

—DR. CRAWFORD W. LORITTS JR., author, speaker, and senior pastor
of Fellowship Bible Church in Roswell, Georgia

"Once again Dan Allender has propelled us headlong into the paradoxical wonders of the gospel of God's grace. *Leading with a Limp* exposes the thin veneer of respectability we leaders try to stretch over our destructive idols of control and pragmatism. In so doing, Allender invites us to the freeing humility of leading as "the chief sinner" in whatever context God has placed us."
—SCOTTY SMITH, founding pastor of Christ Community Church
in Franklin, Tennessee, and coauthor of *Restoring Broken Things*

"I often wonder if other people feel the way I do when they read books on leadership. Most of the books are heavy on motivation or strategy or positive thinking. Dan Allender looks at how anyone can move his team—and himself—forward when he is pummeled by circumstances and his heart is fainting. This is real-world stuff, but you'll have to take off the rose-colored glasses to read it."
—BOB LEPINE, cohost of FamilyLife Today

"*Leading with a Limp* will have a lasting impact on me; it addressed several issues I'm struggling with at this point in my life and leadership. I thank God for this honest and insightful book!"
—BRIAN MCLAREN, pastor and author of *The Secret Message of Jesus*
and *A New Kind of Christian*

LEADING
WITH
A LIMP

Take Full Advantage *of* Your Most Powerful Weakness

LEADING
WITH
A LIMP

DAN B. ALLENDER, PhD

WATERBROOK
PRESS

LEADING WITH A LIMP

All Scripture quotations, unless otherwise indicated, are taken from the Holy Bible, New International Version®. NIV®. Copyright © 1973, 1978, 1984 by International Bible Society. Used by permission of Zondervan Publishing House. All rights reserved. Scripture quotations marked (NLT) are taken from the Holy Bible, New Living Translation, copyright © 1996. Used by permission of Tyndale House Publishers Inc., Wheaton, Illinois 60189. All rights reserved.

Trade Paperback ISBN 978-1-57856-952-6
Hardcover ISBN 978-1-57856-950-2
eBook ISBN 978-0-307-55034-7

Published in the United States by WaterBrook, an imprint of the Crown Publishing Group, a division of Penguin Random House LLC, New York.

WATERBROOK® and its deer colophon are registered trademarks of Penguin Random House LLC.

Allender, Dan B.
    Leading with a limp : turning your struggles into strengths / Dan B. Allender.— 1st ed.
      p. cm.
    Includes bibliographical references.
    1. Leadership—Religious aspects—Christianity. 2. Failure (Psychology)—Religious aspects—Christianity. 3. Integrity—Religious aspects—Christianity. I. Title.
    BV4597.53.L43A45 2006
    253—dc22

            2006003516

Printed in the United States of America
2019

20th Printing

Mike and Myra McCoy,
your grace with my failing has invited me to be more in love with Jesus.

Contents

ACKNOWLEDGMENTS

L eading is as natural to me as going to the dentist. I don't have to be told to go fly-fishing or sailing. I take the opportunity to do so whenever the moment is available and the elements are conducive. The same is not true for leading. I have known a few who seem to lead with elegance and ease, but they confess that the price is high and the ability is not innate.

In fact, what I have learned from those who lead well is that the price always seems to outweigh the gain, but to do anything else would be to betray their calling and deprive those who hunger for their wise care. I am deeply grateful for those who have led me to lead and wrestled with me to become a holier and wiser leader.

MIKE MCCOY

As chairman of the board of Mars Hill Graduate School since its inception, you have been a gentle father, bold warrior, and passionate artist who has called each of us to honor our better angels and to confess and repent of our darker paths. You have been a friend who has suffered my failures with Resurrection hope. This book, and certainly the school, would never—and I mean *never*—exist without your care. And thank you, Myra, for leading Mike in the high call of broken leadership.

RON CARUCCI

You are a generous, kind, and wise man who has willingly chosen what still must seem like an absurd path toward being the chief operating officer of Mars Hill Graduate School. Your ability to help others walk into the magnificent calling of God is a work of awesome beauty. Your wisdom regarding the organization of this book was the turning point in its completion. What good is to be found on these pages is to your credit, and truly the failures are mine alone. Thank you, Barbara, for calling Ron to see the wildness of his own calling to be at Mars Hill.

PAST AND PRESENT BOARD MEMBERS OF MARS HILL GRADUATE SCHOOL

Brian McLaren, Kevin Shepherd, Kim Hutchins, Scotty Smith, Ron Carucci, Mike McCoy, Sigi Gbadebo, Barbara Giuliano, Jack Easterling, Ivy Beckwith, and Tim Conder: you have walked with me through one of the oddest and most difficult seasons of my life. There have been numbing losses and resurrecting mercies. The countless conversations, tears, and prayers that you've offered for the sake of this wild dream are a fortune held for us all in eternity. From my deepest awareness of God, I thank you.

RON LEE

As my editor you have led with a prescient voice as a wise father. I am so grateful for your humor and steady hand.

MATT BAUGHER

As my agent and the author of the companion volume, I watch your enormous skill as a leader, writer, agent, musician, friend, husband, and father—and marvel at the goodness of God in allowing a limping man like me to work with you.

LISA FANN

I have no idea in the universe how I could write the book *To Be Told* and forget to thank you for writing the *To Be Told Workbook*. I sometimes wonder if

I will forget where I am buried. Your forgiving kindness and co-labor in our story workshops is a constant reminder of God's goodness.

MY GLORIOUS WIFE, BECKY

My love, no one has called me to suffer with hope and joy more than you have. Your profound passion for prayer and for following Jesus is the surest and truest presence of holiness I know on this earth. These hard and glorious years could not have been weathered without your odd laughter and kind tears. You have led me to Jesus more often than any man has the right to be redeemed.

What Are You in For?

The assumption that guides what you are about to read is simple, yet for some reason it is almost always left unsaid. And when it *is* said, it is hinted at in terms that are far too polite and too highly polished. As a result the hints are not heard.

But this assumption is far too important for us to settle for window-dressing, for sugarcoating. So here's the hard truth: *if you're a leader, you're in the battle of your life.* Nothing comes easily, enemies outnumber allies, and the terrain keeps shifting under your feet. If you've already tried the "easy" solutions, you have found that they come up empty. I know unvarnished truth like this is never easy to hear, but it's the only truth that will help you lead with inner confidence.

And you need confidence because nothing is more difficult than leading. Nothing else in life compares to the hardship of firing a friend or telling people that their work was necessary for a season but their employment has now reached an end. The graduate school I lead has been threatened with lawsuits, and my reputation has been sullied beyond repair by disgruntled employees. At times, the cost of leading an organization doesn't seem that different from the slow, insidious attrition of trench warfare.

Yet I have stumbled on moments of glory in the process of leading, moments that come from remaining in the game despite the apparent absurdity and incredible personal cost. At times all systems have hummed harmoniously—but only after days, if not weeks, of metal grinding against metal. At other moments complete failure has been imminent: the graduate school came within inches of being closed down because an absurd law was reinterpreted by a state employee who had just taken over the job from her predecessor. (The predecessor, in fact, had worked to help us succeed.) A stay of execution came at the last moment, giving us a chance to mount a defense that eventually prevailed.

Grace. Loss. Fortune. Hardship. Victory. Sometimes the worst seat is the best seat in the house, and it comes as a result of leading. I have been asked many times if I would repeat the process of starting a graduate school. I've said, "Never. I don't hate myself that much." Yet while I have no regrets, I do have much grief and brokenness to show for the effort. The bottom line is simple: it is in extremity that you meet not only yourself but, more important, the God who has written your life. It is through leading that I've known the greatest need for a deep, personal, and abiding relationship with Jesus. I wouldn't trade that for all the money, fame, glory, and honor in this life. I suspect the same is true for you.

You may wonder how you arrived at your leadership position. You may wonder even more if you can continue in it. You may also be at war with wanting to be successful no matter the cost. But if you will ponder the call of your loving God as the core of your labor and life, I believe this book will guide you to a new and profound joy in leadership.

Leading is very likely the most costly thing you will ever do. And the chances are very good that it will never bring you riches or fame or praise in exchange for your great sacrifices. But if you want to love God and others, and if you long to live your life now for the sake of eternity, then there is nothing better than being a leader.

THE CORE ASSUMPTION

Since we're talking straight, let's cut to the core assumption upon which everything else in this book is built: *to the degree you face and name and deal with your failures as a leader, to that same extent you will create an environment conducive to growing and retaining productive and committed colleagues.* Sometimes the quickest path up is down, and likewise, the surest success comes through being honest about failure.

This is definitely not an easy path, but consider the alternative. If you don't have the capacity to confess, acknowledging in real time how much you mess up, the result will be a workplace that becomes more cowardly and employees who grow more self-committed, more closed to you and to one another, and more manipulative. They will look out for themselves, not for you or the organization or their colleagues.

The leader's character is what makes the difference between advancing or de-centering the morale, competence, and commitment of an organization. The truth about confession is that it doesn't lead to people's weakness and disrespect; instead, it transforms the leader's character and earns her greater respect and power. This is the strange paradox of leading: *to the degree you attempt to hide or dissemble your weaknesses, the more you will need to control those you lead, the more insecure you will become, and the more rigidity you will impose—prompting the ultimate departure of your best people.* The dark spiral of spin control inevitably leads to people's cynicism and mistrust. So do yourself and your organization a favor and don't go there. Prepare now to admit to your staff that you are the organization's chief sinner.

But there is more. Much of the current literature on leadership is swelled with the notion of self-disclosure, the importance of authenticity, and the need to own one's weaknesses as a means of bolstering credibility. To connoisseurs of leadership literature, this is nothing new. What I am calling you to, however, is far more than the mere acknowledgment of your shortcomings. I'm suggesting an outright dismantling of them—in the open and in front of those you lead.

THE CHALLENGE

Leadership is far from a walk in the park; it is a long march through a dark valley. In fact, leadership has been described as wearing a bull's-eye on your chest during hunting season. Crises erupt at the least opportune moments, many times the result of poor preparation, a lack of planning, or faulty execution.

Your people will keep messing up just like you do. And, yes, every crisis involves people, will be managed by people, and will be resolved—or intensified and prolonged—by people in your organization.

Few crises—and even fewer of your routine decisions—will be simple. Complexity is the byword of our day. Each decision you make is a jump into the unknown, creating challenges that cost your organization time, money, and possibly morale. Few leaders escape the second-guessing or, worse, the adversaries that materialize in response to their decisions. Many times conflict escalates into assaults and betrayal—with the heartache that comes when confederates turn against you. No wonder leaders feel exhausted and alone. No wonder they suspect that other members of the team are withholding the very information they need to make better decisions. No wonder the intensity of the challenge causes so many to burn out or quit.

I won't be so naive as to say the long, dark valley of leadership can be avoided simply by learning to name your failures. In fact, new and, at times, more difficult challenges will arise simply because you begin admitting your status as your organization's head sinner, *and* the normal challenges will remain whether you confess your flaws or try to hide them. But realize that most leaders invest too much capital obscuring their need for grace, which not only keeps their staff at arm's length but also subverts their trust and steals energy and creativity they could otherwise devote to the inevitable crises that continue to arise. And, perhaps even more dangerous, hiding failure prevents leaders from asking for and receiving the grace they most desperately need to live well, not to mention lead well.

THE WORST REASONS TO HIDE

Why is it so rare for leaders to name their failures? What keeps leaders trapped in a siege mentality, cut off from the data they need in order to make better decisions? Three primary reasons—fear, narcissism, and addiction—come immediately to mind. If you are convinced that none of these affects your ability to lead, keep reading. You very likely will change your mind.

Fear

Most leaders avoid naming their failures due to fear, and fear is a completely understandable motivator. If a leader were to openly acknowledge that he is frequently mistaken, that he is deeply flawed, and that he will continue to miss the mark on occasion, the ramifications could be disastrous. A leader with that much candor could lose the confidence of his staff, his clients could take their business elsewhere, and his board could fire him. At least those are the fears that keep us silent.

But what actually does happen when we overcome this fear and come clean about our personal flaws? What happens when we begin to name our cowardice and admit our inclination to hide? Paradoxically, when we muster the courage to name our fears, we gain greater confidence and far greater trust from others.

Still, confronting your fears involves risk. In certain environments any honesty about one's failures can be the kiss of death. So if you love truth and are bound to its proclamation, flee the cults of pretense and Christian artifice. Seek out a new context in which to lead. If you find a church or organization that is not bound to pretense but might simply be ill equipped to admit what the Scriptures teach about our struggle with sin, you will be in a place where honesty has the greatest potential to alter the culture of latent deceit.

Narcissism

A second reason we hide is narcissism. It takes humility to name our narcissism, and we're too married to our image to come clean about how messed up we are. This focus on self strangles authentic confession.

What happens, then, when we finally find a way to divest ourselves of image and ego? When at last we admit flaws and failure, we gain a stronger personal center and greater peace. Fitness experts have emphasized the importance of "core" strength for years. Core strength is like the hub of our strength, and it is far deeper than our stomach muscles. Therefore, core strength isn't gained by doing a few or a thousand crunches; instead it grows to the degree we work at creating disequilibrium while we exercise. A set of push-ups now includes holding a small ball in one's hand while going down, and while coming back up rolling the ball to the other hand. Disequilibrium requires more core strength in order to return the body to balance.

The first set of push-ups to build core strength feels like one is balancing on a rocking deck of a wave-swept boat. It feels uncomfortable and awkward. But in time the rhythm of disequilibrium intensifies our capacity to find a new sense of balance and strength.

Our attempt to not feel off guard actually leads to greater self-absorption and the foolish conviction that we can control the world. True core strength is willing to feel helpless and disturbed, and it results in a self-disciplined and passionate life rather than in a controlling life that fears what may surprisingly arise.

The lie of narcissism is that we can control a world that is spinning out of orbit by narrowing the field of ambiguity into a simplistic perspective. We choose this perspective—a path of rigidity and dogmatism that limits options and lets us deny complexity in the world. We do this even though complexity is inevitable, and no leader will succeed if she closes herself off from it. Only by letting go of dogmatism and embracing complexity can a leader open her mind to a greater capacity for creativity, leading to success.

Addiction

Finally, the beleaguered leader can easily isolate himself and fill his loneliness with the cancers of addictive substances and behaviors, ranging from sex to alcohol to simple workaholism. To avoid this trap a leader must name his loneliness and his tendency to detach from others, then leave behind the addictions that promise to fill the void. Only then will his heart be freed both to receive and to offer care. The result is a healthier and more humane person, well connected with others in authentic relationships, not to mention a more confident and powerful leader who enjoys the benefits of having others invest in his life.

Every one of your weaknesses is the doorway not only to better character but to leadership dividends so enormous that avoiding the necessary risk is utter foolishness. So face your fear, your narcissism, and your addictions, and begin to enjoy the freedom, the peace, and the power of leading with a limp.

THE COST AND THE BENEFIT

The Bible offers this central paradox about life: If you try to keep your life, you are fated to lose it. If you give up your life, you will find it.[1] Whether you believe the Bible or ignore it, whether you think it's a collection of wisdom or insanity, you can't deny the irrefutable logic in the paradox of giving up your life in order to find it.

Think about trying to fall asleep: the harder you try to nod off, the longer you stay awake. Or say you forget someone's name. Ransack your brain trying to come up with it, and seldom will the name appear. But stop thinking about it, and often the name will surface. Even these simple examples reveal that life requires surrender for us to gain what we desire.

Leadership falls in this category, and leading with a limp will definitely cost you something. The cost involves naming some very painful realities about life and leadership, about others and yourself. Perhaps in these pages you had hoped to find pithy, uncomplicated steps guaranteed to turn your work and your personal life around. Get a grip. If life worked that easily, no one would need a book on leadership.

Life and leadership are anything but simple, immediately rewarding, and pain free. Leaders must deal with what is, not the rosy fantasy that we'd prefer.

To find life, you have to lose it. To broaden your effectiveness, you have to narrow your focus. To grow in confidence, connectedness, and success, you have to admit for all to hear that you are a failure. Remember that this truth does not define success the way we've been taught, yet it is the only path to authentic success as a leader.

Few leaders operate out of confidence built on anything but the crumbling foundation of arrogance. Few know peace that is not dependent on performance. Few exercise freedom and creativity that are not bound to conventionality. And few possess the capacity to care for people that is not shadowed by either the urge to please others or to knuckle under to the tyranny of "should."

Take a different path. As an act of leadership, consider the risk of giving up your life through facing, naming, and bearing your weaknesses, and imagine the paradoxical yet promised benefits. Let's walk into that reality, but it's imperative to remember that all movement into reality requires enormous faith.

THE LEADER'S THREE-DIMENSIONAL LIMP

Given the chaos and complexity of leadership, there is no straightforward chart that can offer an accurate visual representation of the primary leadership challenges and the most effective responses to each of them. The challenges do tend to be universal, but the solutions vary according to the leader, the organization, the circumstances, the makeup of the team, and multiple other considerations. Plus, a solution that is presented as the best response to chaos, for instance, might end up being, in your context, the best solution to loneliness or betrayal.

Maybe if these words were printed on a cube and not on flat sheets of paper, I could come closer to creating a chart that would adequately present not only the challenges of leadership and the various solutions but also the multiple combinations and pairings of effective ways to address each challenge. As it stands, however, I suggest that you picture a Rubik's Cube as you look at the charts to follow. The process of limping leadership is so organic, so paradoxical, and so multifaceted that you would need a chart that could be folded, turned, twisted, and realigned in many different combinations to get the full meaning and complete application of what follows.

LEADERSHIP CHALLENGES AND FAULTY RESPONSES

Leadership Challenges	Typical Ineffective Responses				
	Cowardice	Rigidity	Narcissism	Hiding	Fatalism
Crisis					
Complexity					
Betrayal					
Loneliness					
Weariness					

Five universal challenges that every leader faces are listed on the vertical axis. Just as it is essential to recognize these challenges, it is also imperative that you identify your default response to each. The most common ineffective responses are listed on the horizontal axis.

Typically, when facing the problem of complexity, a leader will default to rigidity. By doing so, he narrows the available options in an attempt to bring order and sanity to the complexity he faces. But such a response cuts the leader off from the wide range of options that he needs in order to effectively address the problem of complexity.

While rigidity tends to be a leader's typical response to complexity, it's also true that many leaders respond by hiding or with some combination of the ineffective responses listed. Look again at this chart and consider the five challenges of leadership. As you think about each one, assess and note how you automatically tend to respond to it.

LEADERSHIP CHALLENGES AND EFFECTIVE RESPONSES

Leadership Challenges	Options for Effective Solutions				
	Courage	Depth	Gratitude	Openness	Hope
Crisis					
Complexity					
Betrayal					
Loneliness					
Weariness					

Again, the challenges that every leader faces are listed on the vertical axis. Now, as you think about each challenge, look at the effective responses (on the horizontal axis) that are needed.

Typically, when faced with complexity, a leader needs to avoid rigidity (see the chart on the previous page) and instead draw on depth. At the same time, other effective responses might also be needed. For instance, to effectively address complexity, a leader might draw on courage or hope paired with depth.

As you read the chapters that follow, refer often to these two charts. Also think about the character trait(s) necessary for responding most effectively to each of the five leadership challenges.

1

A LEADERSHIP CONFESSION

Flight Is the Only Sane Response

I don't pet stray dogs. I was bitten on the hand when I was six. I recall watching this immaculately coiffed collie bound out of a neighbor's yard to greet me. Its elegant, effortless movement mesmerized me. I put my hand out and, in a split second, went from being a dog lover to a child wounded in hand and heart. Since that day I've never fully trusted a foreign pooch. I am dog scarred—a tad suspicious, but still open to man's best friend.

The same is true in my approach to leaders known as pastors. I seldom pet a strange or even a well-known pastor. This came about after I was bitten at age twenty-six. As a lowly intern in a local church, I was earning a whopping fifty dollars a week for services that included leading a Bible study, visiting church members, and walking the senior pastor's dog. I worked with the pastor for more than a year, and after I graduated from seminary, I came back as an assistant pastor.

The senior pastor and I often played tennis together, and after one afternoon match, we sat and talked about some of the things he wanted me to tackle in the coming year. He was my mentor, and I was his apt disciple. But it is also true that even though I had graduated from a fine seminary, I had the maturity of a street kid who had barely escaped death, jail, and excessive brain damage due to illicit drugs, and I had little idea how to function in the business of organized religion. The church was as foreign to me as the Junior League.

I was grateful beyond words to have a job and a future with this man and his church. We left the tennis court at five o'clock and reconvened in an elders' meeting at six. An hour into the meeting, the senior pastor said to the leaders of our church, "I've come to the decision that it is best for Dan and the church to part ways." He offered no explanation. It was a clean, simple bite. Several of the elders felt the decision was abrupt and without due diligence, so I kept my job for another eighteen months. But the handwriting was on the wall.

Leaders are dangerous. They can bite without provocation, or at least without logic, and it is best to stay out of their way or you'll have to deal with the consequences. Leaders can seem capricious, aloof, narcissistic, and self-interested. I wanted little to do with their world, so I left the complex world of church politics and the rough-and-tumble culture of leadership to work on my doctorate. But I didn't escape political turmoil.

The academic realm involves politics similar to the clan warfare of early marauding tribes. It is all about loyalty—allegiance to the tartan, flag, and set of convictions that mark your community as unique. If you can wield a broadax or sword well enough and speak the language of the clan, your position is secure until death. This is called tenure. I entered the clan convinced that I would never again lead any group, community, church, school, or sports team as long as I lived. In fact, one of the great advantages of being an academic was that I was expected to complain about the administration, but I didn't have to take on any leadership responsibilities beyond teaching my classes.

Umpteen years later, six colleagues and I wrestled with the decision of whether to apply for accreditation for the graduate school we had haphazardly started in Seattle. We were in a quandary: The school that had allowed us to be a branch campus no longer wanted us. If we chose to disband, we would face humiliation as well as the possibility of lawsuits stemming from the school's inability to fulfill its promise of offering degrees. We decided to apply for accreditation. The application required the signature of the school's president—a position we had never discussed. We really didn't think we needed a president because we planned to operate as a nonhierarchical guild of peers without a central, decision-making figure. We would be a community, not an organization.

When the moment came for the president to sign the application, all heads in the room dropped, including my own. An awkward half minute ensued, and I looked up. Someone noticed my movement and said, "You are the oldest and the best known." I said, "Okay, but you all know I'm not really the president." Everyone laughed. It was as obvious as a scream in the ear: I'd take the title, and we would all share the power and responsibility.

The dream of a nonhierarchical community of peers collapsed under conflicting expectations, bruised feelings, immorality, and—thank God—a board that intervened and began naming failures upon failures, and called us to become an organization and leaders. We've been in the process for six years, and I am still president. I don't deserve to be. Perhaps that is one of the reasons I am still asked to serve in this capacity.

Everything I despised in other leaders I have replicated in our organization. Many times I have acted precipitously in panic before gathering sufficient data. Many other times I have failed to act at all. If in one circumstance I act too slowly, it seems that I act too quickly in the next. Leadership feels like playing the slot machine in a casino. You put your best capital into the machine, pull the lever, watch the wheels spin, and come up empty handed. The question lingers: what am I doing wrong?

My colleagues and I have gone through enormous heartache and tremendous change. We are still in the middle of profound transformation, and there are days I wonder if I will survive to see the sun rise again. Last night I tossed myself through a midnight aerobics workout that continued to the early side of three o'clock in the morning. I worried, prayed, and thought about personnel matters, finances, future hires, the school's reputation in the community, tensions among the faculty, and a host of other concerns that zapped my mind like moths flying into a bug light.

No doubt every leader feels the constant and chronic weight of obstacles, but it isn't one problem or even a whole set that eats our lunch; it's that each problem requires a response that seldom resolves the issue. Instead, the response simply creates multiple new problems. The weedlike problem seems to have a pod stuffed with countless seeds that will be sown the moment it is pulled, seeds that will result in a host of new weeds. And if that trouble isn't hard enough to swallow, the real issue is more personal—having to do with the decisions and choices a leader must make, alone.

Few decisions are simple. In fact, simple decisions are better called choices. Do I want to eat now or wait for my wife to get home? Do we cancel classes when there is a foot of snow in Seattle? We make choices every day that require little thought, have few consequences, and are completed without much need for reflection or counsel. Leaders choose daily, but the real weight on their shoulders lies in the need to *decide*.

And there are no easy decisions. To decide requires a death, a dying to a thousand options, the putting aside of a legion of possibilities in order to choose just one. De-*cide*. Homo-*cide*. Sui-*cide*. Patri-*cide*. The root word *decidere* means "to cut off." All decisions cut us off, separate us from nearly infinite options as we select just one single path. And every decision we make earns us the favor of some and the disfavor of others.

Budgetary decisions, for instance, seldom involve equal distribution of the finite resource we call money. The child who begins college may require most of a family's disposable income. As a result, the rest of the family can't take their summer vacation to the mountains. The decision blesses one and alienates others.

A good leader will, in time, disappoint everyone. Leadership requires a willingness to not be liked, in fact, a willingness to be hated. But it is impossible to lead people who doubt you and hate you. So the constant tug is to make the decision that is the least offensive to the greatest number and then to align yourself with those who have the most power to sustain your position and reputation in the organization.

Leadership is not about problems and decisions; it is a profoundly relational enterprise that seeks to motivate people toward a vision that will require significant change and risk on everyone's part. Decisions are simply the doors that leaders, as well as followers, walk through to get to the land where redemption can be found.

Flight Is the Only Sane Response

There are two common stories I hear from students who come to Mars Hill Graduate School. One group of students will say, "I didn't want to be here. I was working in Washington DC/Portland/Charlotte/Chicago. I loved my job, my church, and my friends, but in a matter of months my life was turned upside down. It felt like God spun me around, headed me west, and here I am, not really sure why. But I am here, and I sense that this is where I am meant to be."

The other group will say, "I knew this is where I wanted to study. I heard about the school through a book/a seminar/a student, and I have wanted to be here for years. But since I've come, I feel like I'm going through a crisis of confidence. I don't know if this is really what I am supposed to do. I'm afraid, and I feel crazy for ever thinking I wanted to come here."

Doubt is the context for surrender. And flight is the path for obedience. When we're reluctant to lead, doubting ourselves and our call, we are ripe for growth as a leader. Likewise, when we hear the call to lead but we run in the opposite direction, God has a way of having us thrown off the boat, swallowed by a large fish, and spit onto the shore where we are to serve. If the situation weren't so serious, it would be hilarious. God invites us to run and yet to know that he will arrive at our place of flight before we arrive so he can direct our steps again.

Perhaps you doubt this is true. Or, more likely, you hope it might be different for you. But the data from the Bible seem to support this premise more often than not. God seems to choose leaders who don't want to serve, and when they do follow God's call, they often do so in a way that creates new chaos. Consider each of the three patriarchs: Abraham was a liar and a coward. Isaac, the least troubled of the three, was forced to live with the memory of his father's knife at his throat, and later he allowed his wife to manipulate the entire house-hold. Jacob was so manipulative and self-serving that he was like Pigpen in the *Peanuts* comic strip, billowing chaotic dust wherever he went.

Or think about Moses. In a ridiculous encounter, God speaks to Moses from a burning bush. Moses removes his sandals and acknowledges the place to be holy ground, yet he second-guesses God's command that he return to Egypt to free his people. (No doubt Moses was recalling his first effort to free the slaves—the murder he committed, a crime which sent him into a forty-year exile.) Moses' efforts to dissuade God led to a second plan that involved Aaron, his more articulate brother. This is not the behavior we would predict of Moses or God. It seems much closer to a script from Monty Python than *Ben Hur*.[1]

God's habit of calling reluctant leaders gets even odder. He calls young Jeremiah, a boy who is no more than eighteen years old. Jeremiah resists three times and secures a promise that God will protect him. As the story unfolds, we see that it would have been wise for Jeremiah to have pressed for a defini-tion of *protection* and then read the fine print. His life was one of inexhaustible suffering and the absence of what most sane people would call protection.

And then there is Jonah.

Jonah is a world-class model of trying to flee the call of leadership. He runs away on a boat and is thrown into the deep chaos of the sea only to be swallowed by a piscine taxi that spits him onto the shore of the very place he was trying so hard to avoid.[2] Again, it is a bizarre story that makes our devo-tion to formal, academic preparation for leadership seem like it was invented on the dark side of the moon.

The kind of people God calls and their reluctant responses to that calling are not what we expect of professional leaders. We expect our leaders to eagerly and faithfully execute their duties. After all, they're trained professionals.

THE FLAWED FORMAL-TRAINING PROCESS

The training process for leaders—secular or religious—can usually be broken into three areas: content, skill, and ethics/character. At the seminary I attended,

90 percent of the curriculum was devoted to content, 10 percent focused on skill, and our character and ethics, or how we lived in relationship with others, was never addressed beyond a few talks in chapel. It was assumed that who we were as people and how we related to others had been addressed prior to our arrival at seminary.

The place for personal growth was thought to be the church, not the seminary. The seminary trained men and women in the Bible, theology, church history, and other academic rigors, and then it taught those who would pastor how to preach and conduct themselves in the church. Practical skills were assumed to be learned from classroom input and field experience. We all knew that what mattered was how well we did on papers and tests.

In the latter part of the twentieth century, however, seminaries began to admit that their students needed much more. So professors of practical theology, who had been or were still in the "real world" of the pastorate, taught courses and occasionally took students into the trenches. But the focus was still about 80 percent content, 15 percent skill, and only 5 percent ethics/character, with a course on spiritual formation thrown in for good measure.

Oddly, the same is true in many MBA and other leadership programs. Content is king. In MBA programs, however, skills are wed more to the curriculum than in most seminaries. Yet character is equally ignored. As more business dishonesty and illegalities occurred and became public knowledge, though, a cry rose to bring in ethics. The secular world has also been quicker to include psychology and its offspring in the mix. Most MBA graduates have studied personality profiles and data on their own work personalities. Folks who have been trained in or who have taught in the business world tell me that the mix is now likely 65 percent content, 30 percent skill, and 5 percent ethics.

Notice the pattern: teach theory and skill, and hope that somehow the issues of character and ethics will take care of themselves. The assumption is that parents have already dealt with their children's character issues or that the church, synagogue, or other religious institution will take care of shaping ethics and personal values. The academy is for content and practical skills.

This is a problem because we in academia fail to address the narcissism that drives many leaders. We enable troubled and manipulative men and women to devour their colleagues, their staffs, and their congregations simply because they've passed exams, written papers, matriculated through a degree, and gained the credentials to be called professionals.

THE ALTERNATIVE: GOD'S REQUIREMENT

What should we require of a pastoral candidate, a corporate CFO, or even a representative to the state legislature? What I am about to write is ridiculous. It won't happen in the public and secular realms. It could possibly happen in faith-based contexts, but it is far from the norm. Yet it is the model offered by most of God's leaders in the Bible.

We should bless men and women who have done their level best to escape leadership but who have been compelled to return and put their hand on the tiller. We should expect anyone who remains in a formal leadership context to experience repeated bouts of flight, doubt, surrender, and return. Why would this be God's plan? Why does God love the reluctant leader? Here is one reason: the reluctant leader is not easily seduced by power, pride, or ambition.

Power

A leader inevitably uses his own power, or limits the power of others, to make things happen. And there are as many different kinds of power in an organization as there are people, but two forms are the most common: instrumental and influential. Think of a family. The mother and father hold the instrumental power to control money and the family's schedule, so they plan the family vacation. But the volatile and moody middle child has the influential power to ruin the vacation.

The people in an organization who can hire or fire, set budgets, determine priorities, evaluate performance, and reward success hold the instrumental power. The influential power might be in the hands of a famous faculty member, a brilliant software designer, or the pastor who resigned but remains in the congregation. It is crucial to know who holds the power to set an organization's direction and tone.

A reluctant leader is highly suspicious of people who work to accumulate and hoard power. One of the reasons godly leaders are reluctant is that they have frequently seen power misused to build personal kingdoms. I have several friends who worked in education but were ruined by a bully school superintendent. This individual first emptied the school board of strong voices and then filled the empty seats with yes-men and -women who were not experienced in educational processes. She then began to remove school principals who questioned her authority. In one tirade she yelled at a principal, "I will not tolerate insubordination. You will not scream at me or humiliate me in public ever again." The preceding interaction had been heated, but no one else present at the meeting felt that the superintendent had been treated poorly.

This woman dealt with the school district's multimillion-dollar debt by cutting the programs and the positions of individuals who questioned her, and she rewarded the few who protected and promoted her regime. And there was nothing that the victimized teachers could do. The superintendent covered over her violence with school administrator rhetoric. She marginalized every critic as a miscreant. And because of her dictatorial rule, highly qualified teachers and administrators—the ones who weren't forced out—fled the sinking ship.

Reluctant leaders don't aspire to hold power; in fact, they avidly work to give it away. They attempt this even as they use power to create a context where power is used fairly, wisely, and with checks and balances. A reluctant leader does not hoard power because doing so creates more pressure and demand. Power is like a weighty gold bar. It can't be slipped into one's wallet; instead it must be carried obtrusively everywhere one travels. It elicits the envy of others and many will want to take it. The reluctant leader detoxifies power by empowering others to bring their vision, passion, and gifts to the enterprise. She creates an environment of open debate that honors differences and where no one fears reprisal.

In the leadership approach of a reluctant leader, it is a blessing to give away power and a calling to monitor its faithful use.

Pride

A reluctant leader is not likely to be caught in pride's limelight. Pride is a perverted form of worship. Pride basks in the light of its own glory and blesses its goodness as originating from within. Prideful people, however, never seem secure in their self-evaluation: they require a community to idolize their glory.

Self-glory pushes prideful leaders to remind others of who they know and what they've read and written, of their earned degrees and the programs they have created. Such leaders are seldom wrong, and they always are in the know. Pride is a sucking vortex that, vampirelike, draws into itself the goodness and glory of others.

Such pride is contagious. Being in the presence of a pride-driven soul begets a craving in others for more power. It is like being in a wealthy enclave of Mercedeses, Porsches, and Bentleys when you're driving a Ford. What once seemed like a good car no longer feels adequate. Similarly, the presence of a self-glorifying leader lures with a vanity fair of opportunity. Followers try to do whatever is required to keep their personal stock high and to avoid the danger of crossing swords with the narcissistic leader. This contagion is nearly impossible to escape. The only way out is to flee for one's life.

And a reluctant leader is one who has fled in the past. He knows he is a coward and a fool. He already tried to slip away, but he got caught. He went AWOL and, rather than being court-martialed, was advanced in rank. How does one fathom the absurdity? So it's no surprise that a reluctant leader is not impressed with either his ability or the results of his labor. This quality is why Paul underlined the type of people God calls as leaders. He said, "God chose the foolish things of the world to shame the wise; God chose the weak things of the world to shame the strong."[3] Why? Because such a selection process clarifies who deserves the glory and who is to be grateful just to have been a part of God's story.

A reluctant leader gets to boast in the foolishness of God. It is this wise conundrum that sets the tone for the unique mark of biblical leadership. When something goes well, we are not to say, "It is all of God. He gets the praise. I was just being used by him." That is partly true, but not true enough.

We can more rightly say, "I had a great idea, and I worked like a madman. But left to myself I would have created a nightmare. God turned good, clean bones into dancing flesh." The truth is that I am pretty smart and I work very hard, but the goodness of my creation, just like the breath of my body, is a gift. Can I take an ounce of credit for my mind or for my capacity to endure the high levels of boredom required to get a PhD?

A reluctant leader knows that her calling to lead is ridiculous, but she bears the high glory of God's decision to call weak fools into the work of leading others. Consequently, a reluctant leader smiles at the striving ambition of power-hungry leaders to make more and keep more.

Ambition

The ambitious leader pushes relentlessly to do more, to build a bigger organization, and to attract more notice. Of course the reason for building something bigger is always to do more good for the cause. We can serve more people if we have more staff, more airtime, and more money. But enough is never enough.

It should be clear, however, that the issue of ambition is not primarily a matter of size. There are organizations with thousands of employees that are not driven by ambition. Conversely, I've met leaders of organizations consisting of two people who burned with the frenzy of growth. The mark of ambition is the zeal for bigger, better, and more—no matter the cost to people or the process. The ends justify the means because it is better to burn out than to rust out.

Ambitious leaders sing the vision and spin the cost. Rather than acknowledging what must be sacrificed to move from point A to point B, ambitious leaders extol the need and the benefits of the death march. The ambitious leader has a clean-shaven face, a stylish haircut, and a starched uniform. He plays a military march as his soundtrack, and when anyone questions the timing or wisdom of the plan, that person is viewed as a troglodyte or traitor.

Not so with the reluctant leader. He is more like the battle-weary master sergeant who has trained many freshly minted West Point grads in the realities of their craft. The reluctant leader has been to war and knows that almost nothing justifies sending men and women into harm's way. The reluctant leader knows that perhaps one war out of one hundred is fought for a just cause, so he is not caught up in the hoopla of bigger and better. He refuses to serve the larger good by telling lies to get people involved. When new buildings need to be built or new programs grown, the reluctant leader works hard to minimize the cost to the constituents and looks for every possible way of utilizing space or revising existing programs.

The reluctant leader is not looking for luxury or a large office, nor does she invest in the makings of a kingdom. One way to identify an ambitious kingdom builder is her refusal to plan for succession. There are countless horror stories about leaders of Christian organizations holding on to power late into life. Such refusal to prepare for succession in advance hamstrings the organization from developing high-capacity leaders at lower levels. Meanwhile, the top executive begins to see every potential leader as a rival and a threat.

Perhaps just as destructive as having no plan is the ambitious kingdom builder who aspires for his son to inherit his throne. Seldom is the son equal to the father, and as a result the organization becomes a shell of its former self. There are significant exceptions, such as Franklin Graham, the son of evangelist Billy Graham, but the notable failures are too obvious and plentiful to mention.

The reluctant leader doesn't merely give accolades to others. It is her true joy to see others awaken to their potential and exceed their greatest dreams. It is the hope of every good teacher to have students who take their work further than the teacher was able to do. To be surpassed is the ideal. To be replaced is the goal, not a sign of failure.

These are the hard realities of reluctant leadership. It is a calling that is ridiculous and counterintuitive and paradoxical. And the only sane response is to run as fast as you can in the opposite direction. If you are in fact able to escape to a more private and quiet existence, then count it a blessing of God's kindness. He has decided to spare you the costly experience called leadership.

But there is another possibility. If God is real and involved in your life and wants you to be a leader, he will corner you and direct you back into the good that you are to live. So if God captures you, stop running, count the cost, and lead. The more passionately a leader tries to flee but is cornered by God to serve in leadership, the more clearly she understands that her service is an exposure of her weakness and a revelation of God's goodness. It is God's design to use reluctant servants to usher in glory.

2

WHO IS A LEADER?

Why It's Necessary to First Count the Cost

A leader is anyone who has someone following her. If anyone looks to you for wisdom, counsel, or direction, then you are a leader. If there is one little girl who looks at you and says, "Mommy," then you are a leader. If there are fourteen high-energy boys holding aluminum weapons and screaming that they want to be first to hit the ball that rests on a rubber T-ball frame, then you are a leader.

It takes only one child grabbing your finger with a small, sometimes-trembling hand to signify that you are a leader. And from your child's birth to the day you pass from this earth, you will continue to make life-shaping decisions as a parent. And of course it's not just parents who lead with such power and influence. *Anyone* who wrestles with an uncertain future on behalf of others—anyone who uses her gifts, talents, and skills to influence the direction of others for the greater good—is a leader.

No one is a mere follower. If you are a follower of God, for instance, then you are called to lead. Every believer is called to help someone grow into maturity—and such is the core calling of a leader.

Many of us who lead in a formal capacity have little idea how we got to where we are. Being placed in a position of leadership happens seemingly by happenstance. We have a talent for singing and at some point find that we are

leading a choir. Or we have a love of engineering and wake up one day to realize we are supervising fifteen junior engineers. Most pastors enter the ministry
because of a desire to teach and yet spend the majority of their time and energy
in administration, attempting to resolve personnel conflicts and making
impossible decisions. Finding yourself in leadership may very well be the most
common occurrence of the classic bait and switch. We begin a pursuit—be it
business or art or ministry—out of pleasure and desire. And then, before we
blink twice, we are leading. It isn't what most of us set out to do, and as a result
very few of us enter leadership having first counted the cost.

Few accidental leaders like this would dare call themselves leaders. It seems
either too presumptuous or too dangerous. Yet you are in fact a leader if you
are at the very top of an organization—or at least high enough up to warrant
an official label. Other people are just doing their jobs. But if you refuse to recognize this role and calling as a leader, you will also refuse to face the responsibility, the cost, and the joy of your calling.

WHAT WE REALLY BELIEVE ABOUT LEADERS

We think of leaders as occupying formal positions that influence the shape and
direction of a church or organization. When asked to talk about what enables
a leader to lead, we often use words such as *authority, power, confidence,* or
charisma. A leader has power that sets him above others and gives him the
right to make decisions that shape the way an organization will function.

But savvy connoisseurs of leadership know that good leaders don't rely on
power; they don't impose their will on a group as a fiat. Instead, the process of
exercising authority is far more complex—more consensual and interactive.
But after all the fluff is stripped away and the group processes of discussion
and receiving input and feedback come to a close, someone must decide.
Leadership will always require one person to stand closest to the edge and say,
"Let's jump."

If we're honest, we'll admit that we want that person to be a professional,
an expert. We want that person to be different from us (so we can look up to

him) and yet be similar enough to share our values and our perspective. We are ambivalent about leaders, to say the least.

Consider what we require. First, a leader must be physically attractive. If that sounds superficial and silly, then you are not aware of the research into the effects of physical appearance on people's opinions of us. A therapist who is considered more attractive will have three times the perceived credibility than the one who is seen as unattractive. A communicator who is more physically attractive will be regarded as more knowledgeable and truthful than an average-looking one even if their presentations are identical.

We also presume our leaders will be fluent public speakers with a firm command of their audience. An average speaker with a meat-and-potatoes delivery is not sufficient. We presume that a leader worth following will have panache, a charisma that sets her apart for this task, but of course without being haughty or condescending.

We seek leaders who are well-educated, open, sincere, humble, salt-of-the-earth people able to pull themselves up by their bootstraps, leaders who never forget their humble beginning or the values and convictions of those they represent.

We expect a leader to make tough decisions—to fire his close friend if necessary or to send troops into harm's way—yet we want him to tear up over a sad story and be sentimental on Mother's Day. What we want is an illusion and we know it. We prefer the illusion because we have a deep need to be buffered from reality. Setting up a leader to be our big daddy, our bright and shining knight, our perfect mother who will get up in the middle of the night and hold us until we feel safe makes leadership a nightmare that we inflict on a few while we comfort ourselves that we don't have the right stuff to pull it off.

We're merely the followers who decide when to topple our imperfect leaders. We can walk out of church and complain to our friends about another sermon that just wasn't up to our standards. At a church I once visited in a neighboring town, I heard a man say, "I just don't know why he has to dumb everything down to a point of trying to reach the most immature." I was stunned at such a public assault. And then at coffee I heard another saint say,

"Our pastor always feels like he has to make his sermons so theologically complex. I just wish he would put the cookies on the lower shelf so the rest of us could get it."

I wanted to scream for the pastor of that church. Every week he enters the pulpit with a rope around one arm and another around his leg, and perhaps one around his neck. When he begins his sermon, clusters of his community gather around one rope or another and begin to tug and pull. By the time this pastor finishes a half-hour sermon, he has been drawn and quartered, but he still must greet his people at the end of the service. We require our leaders to be perfect—or at least much more perfect than we are—and then we reserve the right to pick them clean like vultures that have patiently waited for the wounded beast to stop twitching.

Who in his right mind would want to be a leader? And who would admit that God calls *every one of us* to lead? The dilemma is this: God *does* call every one of us to lead. Again, a leader is anyone who is moved to influence others to engage a problem or an opportunity for good. When we get involved with a few friends to encourage our neighborhood to recycle, we are leading. If we are moved to make others aware that children are being sold into sexual slavery, we are leaders. If we teach a Bible study or take a position as a nursery worker, then we are leading. How humble our context for leadership may be is never an issue. If we are being followed by someone who looks to us for wisdom, direction, perspective, or a decision, then we must embrace our calling and lead.

COUNTING THE COST OF LEADERSHIP

Why are we so reluctant to lead? Why do so many leaders quit? Or if they continue in their positions, why do so many then lead with far less passion and joy than when they began? Again, a paradox enters the story. In order to reclaim the joy and passion of leadership, we must walk the valley of the shadow of death and name the cost of leadership. This is true whether you are a pastor, president, or parent; janitor, factory worker, or farmer; youth leader, worship leader, or Bible study leader.

Every leader must count the cost of leadership, and the cost includes six realities: crisis, complexity, betrayal, loneliness, weariness, and glory. No one escapes these twists and turns in the valley.

Crisis

Leadership is a walk on the wild side. If we didn't have to deal with people or problems, leadership would be a piece of cake. Instead, leading an auto dealership, a church, or a seminary is all about moving toward a goal while confronting significant obstacles with limited resources in the midst of uncertainty and with people who may or may not come through in a pinch. Leadership is about whether we will grow in maturity in the extremity of crisis.

Crisis is the eruption of chaos, the cloudburst that ruins the beautiful day. We want fair winds and a safe run from our port to the destination ahead. We may have secured a favorable weather report and prepared the boat for every possible problem, but as sure as the sun will rise, tides will change, and entropy happens, few of our plans will go as we design. There is no way to plan for all the contingencies or have all the knowledge we need to navigate the strange waters of life.

Crisis is not a bump in the pavement that causes us to hold the steering wheel more tightly; it is the wall that we hit while we're steering with everything we've got—and it leaves us wondering how we will survive. Crisis is a context for opportunity and growth, but it also takes us to the edge where some don't survive. Thinking that we remember those who finish second is foolish. The NFL team that wins its division and then its conference championship has achieved a successful season. But once the Super Bowl is over, there are few (other than those who rooted for the losing team) who remember the runner-up. The winning coach will keep his job; often the losing coach will be fired.

Crises serve to remind us that we are fundamentally not in control. In reality, we are dependent on grace, on a host of people and circumstances that operate well beyond our control, and on the perspiration we have expended in trying to anticipate the unknown (an impossible feat in and of itself).

We also have competitors who are constantly at work to replace us. We have adversaries who want not merely to replace us but to destroy us. We have enemies in high places who operate with powers and principalities that wish us hellish harm. We live in a disturbed universe that groans daily like a woman in childbirth, and we share the planet with people who at their best are still a mixture of glory and darkness. We all deal with a finite, fallen, unpredictable world that is bent on decay and moves inexorably toward a final, cataclysmic crisis. As leaders, we live on the edge of disaster each day.

Complexity

As if crises were not enough, all leaders must also deal with competing values, demands, and perspectives. As we handle a crisis or even make a fairly simple decision, we are sucked into a vortex of competing possibilities. Due to a charismatic and compelling preacher, a church grows far beyond its physical capacity. The senior pastor provides his growing congregation with countless amenities that make coming to the church even more rewarding. Youth programs become a tour de force rivaling Disney World. Small groups are offered for age groups, specific needs, and symptom clusters. Worship is a feast of drama, videotape artistry, and Nashville-level professional music. The church booms.

But behind the growth and outward signs of success lies a succession of impossible decisions. Do you spend money on additional staff or on bricks and mortar? Do you divide the congregation and grow a separate daughter church, or do you harness the momentum at one site and operate on the philosophy of scale like Sam's Club? Such decisions go far beyond the pragmatic aspects of developing mission and vision statements and defining operational objectives. Always the bigger question lingers: what is the right thing to do? And if the issue is not a clear matter of right or wrong, good or bad, then are decisions entirely relativistic and random?

And what about personnel matters? How much failure do you endure before releasing an employee? An organization can adopt watertight personnel policies and procedures and still face decisions that would test the fiber of Solomon's wisdom. It is standard operating procedure for church, parachurch, and nonprofit organizations to hold on to employees who are not performing as well as required. And in any start-up organization, some employees who were essential players at the beginning may not be suitable for the next phase of the organization's growth. But who will make the call? Who will set the standards, assess the output, coach the weaknesses, and then eventually decide to advance the person or fire him?

Operating according to biblical principles in a corporate or organizational context—one that is governed by a unique mission and vision, one that faces competing demands and needs—feels like picking where the ball is going to land on a roulette wheel. With the best wisdom available and much reflection and prayer, leaders decide. And often the decision sets into motion the next crisis.

Betrayal

If you lead, you will eventually serve with Judas or Peter. Betrayal in some form is as sure as the sun rising in the east and setting in the west. And somehow the fact that betrayal is inevitable makes experiencing it that much more bitter. It is like looking at the ten people who serve on a committee with you and wondering, *Who will take my words and soak them in kerosene and attempt to burn down my reputation?*

Paranoia? Perhaps, but Jesus endured the betrayal of both enemy and intimate friend. One refused to repent and took his shame and fury to the grave. The other confessed and was welcomed back, instructed to feed his brothers the forgiving love he had received from Jesus. In either case the wound initially feels the same, and the scars remain even when there is confession and reconciliation.

David wrote of the agony of betrayal in profound terms:

If an enemy were insulting me,
>   I could endure it;
if a foe were raising himself against me,
>   I could hide from him.
But it is you, a man like myself,
>   my companion, my close friend,
with whom I once enjoyed sweet fellowship
>   as we walked with the throng at the house of God.[1]

Beyond the loss of relationship and joy is the fear that comes when a friend becomes a sworn enemy. The one who is betrayed will never be able to remember the sweet fellowship of the past without feeling a rip in her heart, and she is unable to consider the future without wondering what is around the next corner. Betrayal marks the past and mars the future. And once a betrayal occurs, it is nearly impossible to escape both self-doubt and self-recrimination: *Why didn't I see it coming? What did I do to deserve it? What can I do to make everything right? Why are things getting worse? Why won't this person believe I meant no harm? Am I as bad as this person says?*

Betrayal always brings with it some distortion of the truth. The betrayer twists the truth to garner more power or position while belittling his rival or his former friend. Part of the helplessness experienced by the victim is the inability to repair the breach and set the record straight. Any effort to do so looks defensive; any failure to mount a defense looks weak. It's a superb bind that feels a lot like twisting on the end of a skewer.

Even when the betrayal is not deep, it still brings harm, and we often fail to take into account the mounting toll of many daily betrayals. For a pastor, it is the couple who leaves the church after five years of involvement. When asked why, they hem and haw and say, "Well, the preaching just doesn't move us like it did. We really need to go somewhere where we are better fed." Pastors are told they have to develop thick skin but keep a tender heart. Yeah, and leprechauns are waiting to offer expert counsel on winning lottery numbers.

Anyone in leadership knows that critique, even when it's meant to help, stings like salt in a wound. At times even the rebuke of an enemy can be the very word of God, but still it sears and wounds us. Betrayal lies at the root of many leadership crises.

Loneliness

There is an old saying in Washington DC: "If you want a friend, get a dog." Few people will ever have a lifelong soul mate, and leadership makes friendships even more perilous. After all, most people who serve in formal leadership have the power to alter another person's work. Each of us is highly invested in our work, and few friendships can endure one person having more power than the other. Even more so, when that power is used to alter a person's work in a way that feels injurious, only one in one billion can prevent that unequal power and authority in the work setting from affecting a friendship.

The data are fairly clear about those at the top of the organizational chart. The higher you are, the more rarified are your friendships. The ones that last over countless crises and conflicts are forged in iron. And those friendships, like true soul mates, are as rare as oxygen at thirty thousand feet. Therefore, one price of formal leadership is being alone. Many who enter leadership are dyed-in-the-wool introverts. For them, being alone is often the preferred path. But even introverts desire connection and engagement in both personal and professional matters.

Leadership loneliness is far more than the state of being alone. The fact that we are set apart for a task and a calling is what deprives us of the normal fare of family and friendship. It doesn't mean there is no family or friendship; leaders simply engage in family relationships and friendships in a different fashion. The perks of position can further divide us from others. The days on the road, often to desirable locations, seem enviable, and sometimes they are. But more often than not, from the leader's perspective, the supposed perks seem paltry compared to the allure of normalcy.

Loneliness also assaults a leader when he must absorb the inevitable expressions of disappointment from others when their legitimate expectations are not fulfilled. These criticisms come in part because leaders, of all people, are so busy they never get enough done, such as responding to e-mail and voice mail. And often they fail to show up at family events and at gatherings with friends. The leader must bear not only the loneliness but also the guilt that comes with knowing others' disappointment. Add that guilt to the weight of the impossible choices a leader must make, and it's easy to see how burdens set the leader apart and make him a solitary figure. Steeling himself against such criticism and guilt is tempting and leads to further separation if indulged. Think about it: the leader is often the only one tossing and turning all night over his decisions and the consequences of his decisions, both of which lead to personal criticism.

Weariness

Look at the face of a U.S. president when he takes office and then at his picture four or eight years later. He ages much faster than the rest of us. Few leaders, no matter what margins they build into their lives, can glide through their labor unaffected. The physical body suffers in leadership. Paul reminds us forcefully and kindly not to be weary in doing well, because in due season we will see the fruit that comes from the harvest of righteousness.[2] He encourages us because he knew that caring for others is demanding; and far more than merely exhausting, it saps our hope. Paul spoke from experience. He sent these words to the Christians living in Corinth:

> We do not want you to be uninformed, brothers, about the hardships
> we suffered in the province of Asia. We were under great pressure, far
> beyond our ability to endure, so that we despaired even of life. Indeed,
> in our hearts we felt the sentence of death.[3]

Paul suffered to the point of despairing of life itself. He knew not to quit, but growing weary and quitting was an option always just within reach. He knew that caring for people and doing so to the glory of God requires more than most mere mortals have to offer. Even more, trudging through sin, calling forth beauty, and persevering in the midst of the long wait to see the seeds of faith germinate and make their way above ground—all of this puts a ton of stress on our capacity to hope.

Weariness is really about this core struggle to hope despite the circumstances and our limitations, and not so much about stress and being tired. Will we continue to pray, dream, and fight for people when the battle looks pointless? When the pallor of death begins to shroud the marriage of a friend or colleague, will we fight to help the couple reconcile? Or will we encourage them to cut their losses since we are too weary and too short on hope?

Paul provides encouragement by assuring us that we will see fruit: we will one day see a harvest of righteousness that will make all the waiting and the daily hoeing and tending of the young shoots worthwhile. We will grow weary; that is inevitable. But in our struggle with despair, will we press forward with the conviction that some glorious eating lies ahead?

Paul found joy in his suffering because he could see that it would take his friends into a new understanding of the suffering of Christ. He also knew that when he offered comfort to others, it became a measure of the comfort Jesus wanted his friends to know. Paul wrote,

> For just as the sufferings of Christ flow over into our lives, so also
> through Christ our comfort overflows. If we are distressed, it is for
> your comfort and salvation; if we are comforted, it is for your comfort,
> which produces in you patient endurance of the same sufferings we
> suffer. And our hope for you is firm, because we know that just as you
> share in our sufferings, so also you share in our comfort.[4]

Glory

One of our greatest struggles as leaders is what to do with glory. A leader who has fought for her son, team, staff, or friend will experience a moment of glory. But the greatest glory we can know is to see Jesus' life planted in a heart and watch beauty and righteousness begin to grow. We can weather long seasons of drought and wicked days of opposition when there are a few moments of resplendent redemption.

But here's the dilemma: it's not easy to be called to the table to eat and drink and dance with God. It is not easy—in fact it is almost intolerable—to experience the white robes of glory blaze in a pinnacle of beauty and then be told we can't stay there. Even worse, after moments of glory, God generally tells us to engage a difficulty that is impossible to handle at our level of maturity and faith. Glory casts us not into ease but into the arms of a relentless God who desires for us to know even greater glory.

The process is like being beguiled by the one-armed bandit called a slot machine. One of the strongest ways to motivate behavior is by intermittent reinforcement. The slot machine randomly spits out ten quarters after a lever has been pulled an indeterminate number of times. Put the quarter in and pull the lever. Put in eight more quarters. Nothing happens. And then with the ninth quarter the three lemons come up, the lights pulse, and the clang of falling quarters fills the casino. And the fool, previously feeling some level of discouragement, is now reborn and newly committed to feed the bandit more quarters.

God works in a similar way. He woos us and we follow him. We pray, we fast, and we give. We urge him to transform our friend or our colleague. We talk to the person; we read the Bible with him and pray. And very little changes. The machine keeps taking our quarters. We keep plugging away, and then out of the blue a seed takes hold. A bit of green pops out of the ground, and the first sweet fruit of new life invites us to party. And we are hooked. More quarters go into the machine, and we remain as confused by how and when God works as we are at the random payout of a slot machine.

Glory is compelling. The more we taste, the deeper its hook in our soul and the harder it is to dislodge the hook and flee from leadership. With all the suffering and struggle involved in leading others, why would we not bolt? For one reason: God pours out enough of his presence to keep us hooked. And God allures us to the point we want to know how the next episode of the story will turn out. God is playing out his plot, and reluctant and limping servants, while being humbled as leaders, are lifted up to see his glory.

3

A Case Study in Successful Failed Leadership

The Isakson Construction Company

Most real learning comes through stories. That's why I think *Leading Minds,* by Howard Gardner, is one of the finest books out there on leadership. It is a thoughtful analysis of the strengths and weaknesses of twelve different leaders, and the author's premise is this: a leader leads by the stories he tells and the myths he creates on behalf of his people. Gardner also argues that the best way to gain access to the nature of how leaders lead is to observe how their personal stories intersect with their professional myth making.

So I want to look at how personal stories shape the way we interact in the professional world. To do this, we'll consider a man who came to lead the family business after a long struggle over the transfer of power. Leaders inevitably face conflict, and observing the relational struggles involved in such conflict reveals a person's character. This story illuminates in particular how events in the business world reveal matters of the heart.

The story of the Isakson Construction Company has been studied in many journals. But I want to consider this well-tracked narrative in the light of family conflict. In business, the passing of the mantle of leadership from one generation to the next is often fraught with complexity. And in a family business, that process can ruin both the family and the business. In the case of the Isakson family, the business plan was clear as to which son was to take over leadership, but the implications of that choice were never addressed in the family.

One consultant on family transfers of power offers this insight:

Founding fathers are more often than not conflicted about their successor sons. (It's too soon to know yet if this syndrome will carry over to daughters.) On one level Dad wants his son to succeed and make him proud and rich, but on another level he may see the son as a threat to his manhood and dominance.[1]

THE ISAKSON CONSTRUCTION COMPANY

Johan Isakson created the second-largest construction firm in the world. His company designed and constructed huge dams, road systems in several countries, and three of the world's ten tallest buildings at that time. A conglomerate, Isakson Construction Company (ICC) handled all facets of its projects: financing, designing, building, and managing both the site and all aspects of the construction process.

Johan announced on his seventy-second birthday that he intended to pass the mantle to a new CEO before he turned seventy-five. He had several sons and many grandsons, and all but the youngest grandsons were possible successors. But the oldest son, Herman, was the heir apparent. He had worked his way up from an entry-level position to senior management. He had successfully managed several of the company's largest projects. He was aggressive, street smart, and resilient. His father favored him and turned to him for both wisdom and companionship.

The second son, Jake, was a computer wiz with an undergraduate degree from MIT and an MBA from Harvard. Brilliant and resourceful, he functioned as his brother's constant and fierce competitor. Herman, if named the company's next CEO, would naturally take the company forward in the same trajectory as his father had done. If Jake, however, were handed the reins, he would divest the company of certain subsidiaries and steer it toward being a shrewder player in international markets. Jake had the backing of his mother.

The most complex and powerful player in this transition of corporate and family power was Johan's wife, Becky Isakson. She did not have an official position in the company, but her ability to influence decisions was widely acknowledged. Those who wanted Johan's business knew that they must court Becky.

She openly criticized her older son, Herman, because he had married a woman whom Becky considered unsophisticated. Furthermore, Becky saw in Herman a proclivity to impulsive behavior, and she feared that ICC would eventually be buried under his lack of foresight and patience. She knew that Jake, with his shrewdness and technological savvy, would take the company into realms that neither Herman nor Johan could ever dream of.

Jake could credit his mother for much of his success. Becky had steered him to technology and had helped him hone his skill for making the best deal possible. She had trained him at an early age to bargain with store clerks, and he had perfected the art of getting a better deal even on items marked with a fixed price. As he grew older, he learned how to arrange discounted financing that no one else could obtain. In many ways it is Becky's machinations that are the pivot point in this case study.

At age seventy-three Johan had a stroke, and the company splintered as the two factions scrambled to claim and control territory. Most of the analysts who have drawn conclusions based on studies of ICC follow the interplay of the sons and the failure of the father to set up a succession plan. But, again, Becky was the real player in the eventual dismantling of the corporation after health issues forced Johan to step down.

FAILED RESPONSES TO THE BIGGEST LEADERSHIP CHALLENGES

A careful look at ICC reveals all five of the biggest challenges that you and every other leader face. And, sadly, the case study of the Isakson family and their construction company illustrates failed responses to each of the challenges. Betrayal was responded to with narcissism; crises were met with cowardice and fear; complexity was shunned in favor of rigidity; loneliness was medicated with manipulation; and weariness was allowed to produce fatalism. A leading international corporation was fractured when the founder's health crisis precipitated a series of common leadership challenges—each of which was addressed by a fatally flawed response.

Betrayal and Narcissism

Becky Isakson came from a proud, powerful, and well-to-do family. Her heritage was blue blood, and her marriage to Johan was a high-society event. But what made this bond so exceptional, especially among families of social prominence, was the love that existed between Johan and Becky. Those who have commented on their courtship confirm that the level of care and respect was impressive.

Eventually Herman and Jake were born. There is little to note about this period other than a sad event in which Johan was caught in a scandal. Here are the general facts: Isakson Construction Company had achieved incredible success but had not yet expanded into the global market. ICC took on several major construction projects that went far beyond the sphere of the company's past success, and in so doing amassed a debt that threatened to sink the company. A competitor began the process of calling in the debt and threatened to take over the company.

Out of desperation to save ICC, Johan "allowed" his wife to become involved with the owner of the hostile company. The details of what happened never became public, but it's clear that Becky was used as a pawn in Johan's efforts to preserve his company. Incredibly, the CEO of the hostile company—the one who exposed Johan's underhanded maneuver—also blessed ICC by giving it a favorable standing in markets that previously had been closed.

ICC became a larger and stronger company, but Becky could no longer trust her ambitious husband. Being betrayed in such a devastating way begets self-absorption. The more wounded a person is, the more she will steel herself against ever suffering such harm again. And the longer the wound is left unattended, the emptier her heart becomes. Becky devoted herself to self-serving and futile behaviors designed to gain back what she had lost.

Narcissism is not merely an orientation to life that is self-centered or self-consumed. It is a far more debilitating process that empties a person's inner core as she becomes more suspicious and manipulative. The wound often energizes a demand to prevail at any cost. The longer the betrayal is unaddressed, the more the wound submerges into the subconscious, and yet it serves as the core motivator for a style of leadership that is brutally aggressive and not open to feedback or any hint of disloyalty. And this type of leader regards even minor criticism as disloyalty.

Years earlier Becky had left her powerful family and fallen in love with Johan. But he had betrayed her, leaving behind a deep emptiness that Becky addressed by allying herself with Jake, the younger son who had failed to earn Johan's favor. The unresolved marital issues led to division within the family and the fracturing of the corporation.

Crisis and Cowardice

The crisis had been brewing long before Johan's stroke. The family knew Herman was favored by his father who had begun to turn more and more of the family enterprise over to his older son's control. The crisis for Becky was her loss of control. At Johan's death or inability to function, she was in line to control vast assets but not the direction of the company. And it was more than money that she sought to control. She didn't want the company to be influenced by the uncouth woman Herman had married. Becky abhorred her daughter-in-law, and she was determined to prevent Herman from running the company. She had begun to position her younger son, Jake, to take over long before Johan's stroke presented the immediate leadership crisis.

It is crucial to remember that for a leader, the current crisis is just another incident in a long queue of previous calamities. As those calamities come, we all develop a style of meeting them. We will respond either out of fear or confidence. Even when a leader looks confident and appears strong, fear may be guiding his operational genius. And the more a leader lets fear be his driving force, the emptier his heart becomes and the more suspicious he is of those with whom he works.

It's a vicious cycle. Fear creates a growing emptiness in the leader, which results in a self-fulfilling loop of paranoia and perceived betrayal. The cycle convinces the leader that she is alone and that the only workable solution is to manipulate the world so she can gain a small degree of safety.

Again, this behavior may appear to be strong and confident, but it is actually cowardly and self-serving. Often it can be masked as a strong commitment to the good of the organization, yet it seldom allows into the process people who challenge the leader's convictions or her way of doing business. Becky's alliance with her younger son was not the care of a loving mother. It was the cowardly control of a woman who had never addressed her wounds or faced the depth of fear that came with suddenly being the wife of a failing husband. The combination of current crises, past wounds, and an uncertain future compelled her to convince Jake to deceive his father and his older brother.

Complexity and Rigidity

Jake's deception was quite simple and even elegant. With him in charge of information technology, the company had made rapid advances in the way business was processed. The more technologically dependent the enterprise became, the less Johan and Herman understood or even cared to know about that area of the company. As long as the operational side of ICC was left in their hands and the systems worked without a hitch, they were happy. What they didn't understand was that the complex operation that Jake had set up controlled much more of the enterprise than they realized.

Jake had created several shell organizations that operated off the radar screen. The big construction projects all came through the doors of ICC, but the technological ability to run the projects, track finances, and hold the records were siphoned off to companies that were solely owned by Jake. The people hired to run those companies were loyal to Jake—or at least to the vast sums of money he paid them without anyone at ICC knowing.

You may recall a simple premise: remembering your lies is more difficult than knowing the truth. The more complex the scheme, the more one needs an ironclad paradigm to house it. The greater the fear of being caught or found out as a person or an organization, the greater the need for subterfuge. We all know life is complex, and the more fear we live with, the greater our need for control. For Jake and his mother, deception became the way to keep life "simple" for them, even though their efforts actually made details that much more difficult to manage.

We all tend to gravitate toward a one-cure-for-all-diseases approach to life. We want answers that work, and whatever works becomes the primary grid through which we see the world. In the case of the Isakson family, the only approach that seemed to work was deceit. The family members never considered gathering all the major players for a heart-to-heart discussion. They never brought in a consultant or a trusted peer. Neither did they submit to their board the process of decision making. Not that the latter would have helped. The board was made up of family members who would not challenge the views of those in power.

When a leader advocates a single way of being, that rigid approach captures all his ways of thinking, squelches spirited debate, silences questions, and forces the way forward along one narrow course. Such rigidity is a form of dogmatism, a narrowing of options that embraces only one way of operating as right and all other ways as dangerous or divisive. Dogmatism is less the nature of what we believe and far more how strongly we hold to our beliefs. A true dogmatist views with suspicion any other approach to a problem because his tried-and-true way is being challenged. Tradition is valued over innovation, and "truth" is used to silence "heresy." What is never asked is how innovation might help him better understand his tradition or how so-called heresy can help him come to a greater understanding of truth. Those answers—those sources of information—are closed to the leader who adopts a rigid stance in an attempt to simplify a complex reality. Such a leader sees all views outside his own as the enemy.

Evidence points to the fact that Becky and Jake fell into this pattern by narrowing their options to just one: the path of deception.

Loneliness and Hiding

If a leader gives in to fear and narcissism and then sets up hierarchies that distance him from staff and colleagues, he will end up with an executive team that is populated by yes-men and -women who are not committed to the good of the organization. The more a leader hides, the more isolated he becomes, and the less information, feedback, wisdom, and true participation he will gain for the best possible decision making. Further, the more a leader hides—the more he is cut off from others in the organization—the more he will need to manipulate others to maintain control.

When isolated leaders attempt to control their destinies, most give themselves over to some process, substance, or person who eases their pain and props up their illusion that they are in control. (This is why many isolated leaders stray into addictions.) Jake and Becky, as an isolated team of two, chose to rely on deception. Jake controlled the lion's share of ICC assets. His subtle act of deception—giving his father only the information he wanted to hear—allowed Jake to consolidate his control over the movement of assets, the storage and retrieval of data, and the processes and procedures that made the business run.

Herman discovered the plot when he wasn't able to move forward with an overseas public works project due to Jake's control of ICC assets. Rumors swirled in the corporate world that Herman threatened Jake's life over it. In the media, however, the threats were reported merely as lawsuits. Herman was known to have underworld contacts, so Jake fled the country. He set up an overseas operation in association with members of his mother's family.

Jake became even wealthier and more powerful, but he lived in exile. In his isolation he also became reclusive, driven, and addicted to work. Eventually he was used and exploited by the relatives with whom he had joined forces. He ended up a mere shell of a man.

Weariness and Fatalism

A requirement of leadership is that we operate at high levels of intensity for lengthy periods of time. The battering waves of crises don't stop, and often the structures that are designed to move us forward break down under constant friction. One breakdown usually exposes the weakness in processes, people, and systems. And new crises are birthed in the face of the precipitating crisis. It's no secret why leaders are exhausted.

In the case of the Isakson family and ICC, the initial crisis precipitated by Johan's stroke spawned additional crises and led eventually to the family's complete ruin. Jake lost his position and his family. Herman lived with rage and a hunger for vengeance. And we know almost nothing about what happened to Becky and Johan. They suddenly disappeared from the public eye. We can only assume that they lived out their years in disgrace after ICC was fractured.

The intensity of leadership produces weariness, and prolonged weariness can easily prompt a sense of fatalism. Ineffective responses to any of the biggest challenges of leadership—betrayal, crisis, complexity, loneliness, or weariness—result in failures that eventually come home to roost. When faced with the consequences of their failure, most leaders sense defeat and become fatalistic. Many who are fired move on to other organizations or ministries, where sadly they repeat the process all over again.

As we draw conclusions from the case study of ICC, we find that we know quite a bit more about Jake than the other principals. But to tell the next part of the story, I must add a level of specificity and detail that makes full disclosure necessary. Jake's name is really Jacob. There is no Johan; his name is Isaac. His wife's name is Rebecca, and Herman is Esau. The story is found in Genesis 25 through 35.

The climax of the story is found in Genesis 32, where Jacob wrestles with God and gains a new name as well as a leader's limp. Prior to the limp, scheming and deceit marked his life. But after wrestling all night with God and gaining a limp that was obvious to all, Jacob in many ways became a different person. His story shows that God intends to wrestle with each of us in order to both bless us and cause us to walk and lead with a distinctive frailty.

The Deceiver Is Deceived

Jacob, whose name means "he grasps the heel" and figuratively "he deceives," stole his brother's birthright and later his brother's blessing.[2] Esau vowed violent revenge, so Jacob fled to his Uncle Laban's home. He went to work for his uncle and soon fell in love with Rachel, Laban's younger daughter. After seven years a wedding was arranged, and following the festivities Jacob slept with his new wife. But in the morning Jacob found that he'd been double-crossed. He had consummated the marriage not with Rachel but with Leah, Laban's older and less-attractive daughter.

Not seeing the joke is impossible. The deceiver has been deceived in the darkness of the night. The blessing has gone to the older daughter, not the younger, and Jacob must keep Leah as his wife. Laban then agrees to give Rachel's hand also—in return for another seven years of work. The time frame keeps expanding, but in the meantime Jacob shrewdly manipulates the herds to enhance his power and wealth.

Eventually, Jacob increases in power and prestige to the point that it causes dissension in Laban's family. Laban's sons begin to squabble about Jacob's success, and the deceiver can see that another crisis is looming. God tells Jacob to flee, and he does, taking his family and his wealth with him and not mentioning to Laban that he's leaving. Laban eventually catches up with Jacob and his caravan. At that point he confronts Jacob about departing in secret. Jacob talks his way out of the confrontation and strikes a peace treaty with his angry father-in-law.

It is a bizarre story. God covers Jacob's tracks as he flees from his deceiver father-in-law. God warns Laban not to harm Jacob, and then Jacob is further protected by a lying wife. (Unknown to Jacob, Rachel had stolen Laban's household gods. Laban searches her tent, but the gods are hidden in a camel's saddle. Rachel uses her menstruation as an excuse not to rise from the saddle in Laban's presence.)[3]

Trying to figure out who is protecting whom through what kind of deception makes the head spin. But the end result is that Jacob wins. He has defeated his father and brother. He has prevailed against his father-in-law and Laban's sons. But Jacob is about to become a new man. He has been set up by the shrewdest player of all: God.

JACOB GAINS A LIMP

Jacob is the third great patriarch of the Jewish and Christian faiths. He is the one whose new name becomes the name of the people, the nation Israel. Jacob's story marks the identity of an entire nation. If stories are one of the primary ways we achieve self-understanding and one of the central means by which leaders create meaning for their organizations, then it is imperative to listen well to the stories that give us a sense of who we are. In this regard Jacob's story is central.

As mentioned earlier, the name Jacob means "deceiver." At birth he grasps the heel of his twin brother and tries to take Esau's firstborn position as they come out of the womb. As a deceiver he must be quick; he must get ahead of everyone else in his opportunistic hold over life.

After fleeing from Laban, Jacob sets out for his ancestral grounds where he will encounter his brother, Esau. Remember, this is the brother from whom Jacob stole the birthright and the blessing, the same brother who swore to kill Jacob. Jacob camps on the side of the Jabbok River in the company of his family and likely a private army. But before the night is over, he sends everyone else across the river and remains alone on the opposite riverbank. Choosing to abandon a safe camp and spend the night without his soldiers is a highly, if not wildly, unusual decision.

Jacob is immediately jumped by a stranger, and they fight all night. The passage is written in a way that indicates this fight is to the bone. It's a life-and-death struggle, but oddly it ends in a stalemate. It might have had an ebb and flow, but neither Jacob nor his rival prevails.

As the first light of day breaks, the stranger ceases the struggle and bids to depart. It is only then that Jacob realizes he has not been at war with a mere man. He is in the presence of an angel or, more terrifying, God himself. The "man" touches Jacob's leg, and the deceiver is permanently marked with a limp. Jacob then asks for a blessing and won't let go until he receives it. The man renames him Israel, meaning "you have struggled with God."[4]

Israel, nee Jacob, then names the place of their wrestling Peniel ("face of God"), "because I saw God face to face, and yet my life was spared."[5] He wrestles with God and comes away broken and renamed. His limp is a reminder that when God renames us, he also makes each one of us a new person through a redemption that requires brokenness.

The process of becoming a person who can lead others with a limp is not what we would have predicted. Do we really have to be that desperate and that deeply exposed to be freed from our narcissism, our fear, our dogmatism, and our tendency to hide? The story of Jacob exalts not the struggle but the goodness of God as he blesses a conniving, undeserving man. No matter how far off the mark we might be, we see in this account the promise that if we open ourselves to meet God, we will not come out of the encounter the same. We will walk a new path—with an unpredictable gait.

It's Failing That Matters!

Nothing Succeeds Like Imperfection

A brilliant and charismatic professor at Mars Hill Graduate School re-signed. The reasons for the resignation could not be discussed then or now, but it was heartbreak for everyone involved. Within a short period of time, various outside accusations were made that ran the gamut from the typi-cal (blaming faculty politics or theology) to petty personal vendettas. Our legal counsel told us to say nothing, but the more silent we remained, the more our students were devastated and incensed.

This resignation came during a period when a number of other staff had left the school. Adding to the tension were miscellaneous rumors and a good amount of confusion related to accreditation issues. All of the administration's efforts to clarify matters and resolve the growing mistrust only seemed to add more chaos and suspicion.

Up to this point the leadership team did what we needed to do, but then we did a stupid thing: we put our heads in the sand and hoped the storm would pass. There were reasons for our ostrich behavior, and at the time they seemed quite sensible. We were near the end of the term, and summer was ahead. Often the summer slows any preceding upheaval, and we hoped against hope that would be the case in this instance. It wasn't.

Students continued to meet and talk. The faculty was exhausted, hurt, and angry, and we all retreated into our own corners to nurse our wounds. Time heals all wounds? This was not the case, at least in the short run. Instead, time intensified the heartache. The infection festered, and by midsummer seven of the eight men and women on the student-leadership team had made plans to leave the school.

. After a vacation, I returned to the school—and sounds of mutiny. Waiting for me was an invitation from the student council to meet for a discussion, and some on the faculty believed that doing so would only create more division. We had not met to talk previously because the administration had been told by legal counsel not to speak. How do you talk when you can't talk? But we were on the border of totally losing the support of the student council and, by extension, many in our student body. I saw this as a make-or-break meeting. If the student council resigned and left the school en masse, I doubted whether our young graduate school could survive.

Now let me offer a little background. As a seminary we had often underscored the importance of honesty and confession as well as the role of story in nurturing community. But the school's leadership had been silenced, so we had refused to enter into conversations either to hear the students' hurt and anger or to confess and narrate what the professor's resignation had been like for us. Now all we had stood for and taught seemed to become a rope to hang us.

The meeting with the student leaders was to begin around six o'clock, and the tension on campus was palpable. I went to talk to Paul Steinke, the student-council president, and in the meeting room I saw a beautiful table set with candles and freshly cut flowers. The students had decided to serve us dinner.

I was dumbfounded. We were invited to sit, and we were served. As we began to eat, Paul spoke, and this is what he said:

> As students we are here with a great deal of hurt and confusion. Some are angry. Some have made the decision to leave the school. Others are in the middle of making a decision about their future, but we all have realized that in our heartache none of us have come to you to ask: how

are you? Whether you have failed or not, we have failed you by not opening our hearts to you and asking what you have endured through these events. We want to ask you to tell your stories, sharing to the degree you wish.

I had come prepared to face their hurt and anger and accusations, and I was wearing body armor to blunt the expected arrows. I was not at all prepared for humility, kindness, and invitation. I nearly started weeping as he talked.

I thanked Paul and began speaking. I don't recall all of what I said, but I do remember crying. I tried honestly to name the fear, the fury, and the soul-deadening silence that I was subjected to bear. I walked them through a place in Montana where I had spent much time with the professor who had left our school. I lost a friend, I lost a river, I lost joy. And I felt that all we had suffered to birth this school was now a bloody joke.

I looked at Paul's face, and tears streamed down his cheeks. Each faculty member spoke a different yet profoundly similar story. We also heard the stories of the students, and our tears didn't abate, but oddly there were moments of unexplained, unplanned laughter. I felt as if I were on a roller coaster coursing through a time warp. At times we traveled the speed of light—images and words flew by faster than I could comprehend them. And at other moments everything slowed to a crawl where words were frozen like breath in subzero cold.

Somewhere during the experience I surrendered. I turned the school and our future over to God. But it seemed far more as if I turned everything over to the dialogue. I gave myself to the words—what I said and what I heard—and I stopped caring about the stuff that brought us to the meeting. I started listening and participating in the heartache of those who spoke.

I can't deny that at moments I felt blamed and became defensive. At other moments I felt impassioned to explain or to offer solutions. But to do so would have been to ruin the magic of the beauty that had been created, so I kept quiet.

Paul and seven other remarkable men and women served us. They heard our stories, and they wept for us. All they asked was for us to do the same. And we did.

The evening did not end with a rousing salute to Mars Hill Graduate School or to the faculty and administration. All wounds were not resolved. In fact, one student said, "This evening was incredibly healing, and I believe you are good-hearted, but it would take an act of God for me to stay." Later he said, "Of course rain is an act of God." After several weeks of prayer, he chose to stay. The future was brighter at the end of the night, but even truer was the fact that a new school was born from the ashes because of the courageous foolishness of Paul Steinke.

LIMPING INTO CHAOS

As the leader of the student body, Paul chose not to retreat. Instead, he created a context for conversation. He chose not to take sides, but neither did he deny his doubts, anger, and heartache. He refused to begin the conversation with accusations. Instead, he served people who at times seemed to be his enemies, and then he gave everyone room to tell their stories. He had counseled, coached, and cajoled the student council and invited them to shape what they wanted to create for us.

Paul is a remarkable leader. He leads by taking the greatest risk of all—inviting dialogue, creating a context for story, living into tension and ambiguity, and blessing chaos as the context for brave souls to find a way through complexity. He doesn't fit the look or style of a modern leader. He is not a consensus-building relational leader who reads the polls and takes people the way they already want to go. Nor is he a smooth autocrat who sets the course and convinces people to follow by the force of his will.

Instead, he is a mess. He invites chaos, jumps into the process, and allows the bumpy road to shake out ideas and options. He knows he can be brash and arrogant, yet he is also tender and kind. He has an odd capacity to trust himself and his senses, yet he is suspicious of himself and open to hearing how others perceive him. He is the leader I hope to be one day. In fact, in many tough moments I have asked myself, *What would Paul do?*

We all need a model. We all need to know how to lead from having watched someone we respect. Leaders are not born, nor are they trained. They are imagined. Indeed, some leaders seem to slide from birth into positions of power, and training can enhance such a person's leadership capacity. However, the guts to lead, fail, and grow come from seeing someone else do what you could not have imagined, but now can.

Before watching Paul lead us through a difficult season, I had not imagined how chaos could birth something good. Before this, I believed that chaos had to be either managed or avoided. But I learned from watching Paul that a leader can enter chaos and call forth the best in others rather than using chaos as a cue for blame and isolation. There were moments in the months following the professor's resignation when Paul spoke words that were hurtful. At other times he allowed the circularity of unaddressed pain to go on too long. No one can enter the tough terrain of leadership and not fail. But Paul did not hide his failures or defend or rationalize his choices. He led in a way that required grace to be more real than his competency.

Prior to this season, I had been aware of some of my deficiencies, but I had never considered that the overwhelming majority of God's hand-picked leaders in the Bible were themselves riddled with faults and failure. I can hardly name a leader in the Bible who didn't fail radically enough to warrant being removed from leadership: Adam, Noah, Abraham, Isaac, Jacob, Moses, David, Elijah, Jeremiah, Mary, Paul, and Peter. It seems God loves to use troubled, odd, unpredictable people to not only lead others but also to make the gospel known.

BEING THE CHIEF SINNER

God loves reluctant leaders and, even better, he loves reluctant leaders who know they are frightened, confused, and broken. In fact, he seems to have a special fondness for rebels and fools. Does God choose troubled leaders because few other people are foolish enough to say yes, or does he choose weak, troubled people because they serve a unique purpose in their broken state? The answer is yes.

God calls leaders to tell a story of redemption through their lives as they lead others in the redeeming story of God. Leaders are primarily storytellers and story makers; and troubled people are called to be leaders because they create and tell compelling stories. Sane, reasonable, play-it-safe people are not sufficiently engaged in life to generate great stories. Instead, they sit back and wait for a leader-storyteller to come along and get them caught up in a life worth living.

Troubled leaders live with their weakness on their sleeve, and it is through their weakness that grace comes to be magnified. Weakness is the big idea of the gospel, which makes it good news for us—who are not terribly healthy, happy, or holy. God's servant leaders are intended to call God's people to repentance and faith. And what better way for God to do so than to first transform the leaders, who are the people who need grace even more than those they teach, encourage, and guide?

The apostle Paul could not be clearer, more direct, or more bizarre. He stated,

> To keep me from becoming conceited because of these surpassingly great revelations, there was given me a thorn in my flesh, a messenger of Satan, to torment me. Three times I pleaded with the Lord to take it away from me. But he said to me, "My grace is sufficient for you, for my power is made perfect in weakness." Therefore I will boast all the more gladly about my weaknesses...in insults, in hardships, in persecutions, in difficulties. For when I am weak, then I am strong.[1]

The story Paul tells is odd. First, as in the story of Job, we have Satan playing a role in the work of glory. Satan afflicts Paul with some wound or suffering—physical, psychological, or both. Paul then pleads with God three times, likely in concert with the three times he is shown glories in the heavens. Paul then hears from God, "Nope. I have a great purpose for your suffering, and that is to reveal the paradox of all leadership: weakness is strength."

This is one of Paul's central statements of inversion. Don't miss this: leadership that mimics Jesus will not be normal. It will be neither expected nor, in most cases, preferred. It will be disruptive and anomalous, and it will demand one's body and soul, fortune, reputation, and all the other small gods that keep our lives safe and satisfied.

Here is God's leadership model: he chooses fools to live foolishly in order to reveal the economy of heaven, which reverses and inverts the wisdom of this world. He calls us to brokenness, not performance; to relationships, not commotion; to grace, not success. It is no wonder that this kind of leadership is neither spoken of nor admired in our business schools or even our seminaries.

The apostle Paul added up all his failures, weaknesses, and sin and called himself the "chief of sinners." In his letter to Timothy, he began the first chapter by excoriating a group of sinners who are some of the most deserving of that title. He named sinners he had never labeled before, including slave traders and mother- and father-killers. Soon after pointing out that the Word of God condemns those who live contrary to righteousness, Paul added,

> Here is a trustworthy saying that deserves full acceptance: Christ Jesus
> came into the world to save sinners—of whom I am the worst. But for
> that very reason I was shown mercy so that in me, the worst of sinners,
> Christ Jesus might display his unlimited patience as an example for
> those who would believe on him and receive eternal life.[2]

In many decades of living as a ragged-hearted believer, I've never heard that passage preached without having the speaker rush to minimize what Paul is saying. Even if it is noted that Paul used the present tense—being the worst of sinners was a *current* reality for him—his sinfulness is seldom spoken of in comparison to the list of heinous sins in the earlier part of the chapter. But this is what Paul was really saying: "Put me up against perverts, killers, and whores, and I beat them all hands down. I was a mess, and I am a mess far greater than any of you. Yet I am your apostle. I am the gospel leader to the Gentiles." In one fell swoop, Paul eliminated the possibility of any leader's serving with even a hint of self-righteousness.

So why do most leaders live in fear that they will one day be discovered and known, exposed and humiliated? They *know* they're a mess, but they hope against hope that no one else will notice.

Paul calls leaders not merely to be humble and self-effacing but to be desperate and honest. It is not enough to be self-revealing, authentic, and transparent. Our calling goes far beyond that. We are called to be reluctant, limping, chief-sinner leaders, and even more, to be stories. The word that Paul uses is that a leader is to be an "example," but what that implies is more than a figure on a flannel board. He calls us to be a living portrayal of the very gospel we beseech others to believe. And that requires a leader to see himself as being equally prone to deceive as he is to tell the truth, to manipulate as he is to bless, to cower as he is to be bold. A leader is both a hero *and* a fool, a saint *and* a felon.

We are both, and to pretend otherwise is to be disingenuous. The leader who fails to face her darkness must live with fear and hypocrisy. The result will be a defensiveness that places saving face and controlling others as higher goods than blessing others and doing good work. Clearly, the biblical model of leadership is odd, inverted, and deeply troubling. It is so troubling that most churches, seminaries, and other religious organizations would never hire a "chief sinner." The only one who thinks to do so is God. Consider the one he chose to lead his people's flight to freedom through the Exodus. There is no question that Moses was his people's chief sinner.

INVERTED LEADERSHIP

Moses was a deeply troubled man, so troubled that—in his opposition to God's stated plan—he vents his rage and, as a result, is forbidden to enter the Promised Land. He was an angry man who began his service in a murderous rage and ended it bearing the consequences of hitting the rock twice in anger. Yet he was the only one who talked with God face to face.

Injustice energized Moses. Although he was a privileged denizen of Pharaoh's world, Moses could not bear to see his people enslaved by a repressive and cruel regime. In a fit of passion, he killed an Egyptian and fled into exile.[3] There he protected a young shepherd girl from being abused by violent men. He was clearly disposed against those who used power with cruelty. Adopted by the shepherd girl's grateful family, Moses spent forty years tending sheep.

Then, after four decades, he was called to leadership—a role that allowed him to continue his war against injustice. In a bizarre encounter with a bush that talked, Moses was told to remove his shoes and begin a dialogue with God. In that encounter God told him what he was to do and how he was to accomplish it. And what follows is so strange that it defies our notion of how God relates to those he calls to leadership. We assume that if God spoke to *us* out of a burning bush and told *us* to do something, we would bow before him and then immediately do as he bid. Not Moses. He stood his ground and fought God's plan.

Moses told God, face to flame, no. "You've got the wrong man because my tongue is slow and thick, and what you are asking me to do is more than I believe I can do." In fact, Moses was probably remembering how his last attempt to save his people had ended. He was a wanted man with a flawed tongue, not a leader of God's people.

Whatever the reasons behind his protest, consider the gall it took to turn down God, who was right there speaking to Moses in the fire.[4] The story makes both God and Moses look strange. If God is so awesome and terrifying, then how does a slow-speaking, tongue-tied shepherd disrupt God's plan so easily? God eventually relents and negotiates a deal that includes using Moses' brother, Aaron, to act as Moses' mouthpiece. Thus, Moses the murderer wins an argument with God.

The story makes me laugh until it catches me by the throat. I laugh in incredulity over a God who argues and debates with his people—until it dawns on me that in the end God wins. But what am I to factor in to my theology from this narrative? How does this story alter my view of God's omnipotence and sovereignty? Without question I affirm that God is omnipotent and sovereign. But what does that mean when I take into account this story, regarding his selection and sending of a leader who was so reluctant to lead that he went toe to toe with the Almighty?

LEADING BEGINS WITH DESIRE

Most leaders had no intention or desire to lead; instead they were thrown into the mess by being discontent. If they had been willing to endure life as it was, then they would never have become leaders. The person who merely puts up with life becomes a manager or a bureaucrat, not a leader.

The difference between a manager and a leader is the internal urge to alter the status quo to create a different world. In that sense leaders are prophets. They see the present as incomplete and inadequate and are willing to risk the comfort of the present for the promise of a better tomorrow. A manager, on the other hand, is content to keep the organization running as smoothly and as efficiently as it can function. A manager serves to keep the plane in the air, whereas a leader wants to put a new engine on the plane midair.

A manager wants to approach the inevitable chaos with the tried-and-true methods that have worked in the past. In contrast, a leader knows that as difficult as it is to bring about change, not to do so will destroy the community. There can be no freedom from the bondage of the daily rut without the chaos that comes with leading people out of the status quo.

A leader who desires nothing more than the status quo becomes an ostrich with its head in the sand. A leader must be troubled and discontent, and he must ask the question, *How can tomorrow be better than today?* He must be a visionary, living in the tension between how to honor what is good and true today and yet be discontent with today in light of what could transpire tomorrow. He is torn between what is and what could be, yet he speaks the future into the present due to his compelling desire for change.

A leader must simultaneously deepen the organization's desire to move while exposing the cowardice and complacency involved in its wanting to remain stationary. A leader offers a prophetic presence as she stirs desire and reminds those she serves what they will lose if they cling to the status quo. Prophetic leaders live in the tension between the past and the future, between the desire to move and the demand to stay. No wonder leading is full of risk and failure. And no wonder leadership requires a person who can own both her fear of moving forward into uncertainty and her inability to remain safe in the sure present.

LEADING BEGINS WITH A SUMMONS TO ACTION

Moses was a leader long before the burning bush sent him on an errand. And he led because he was willing to act. Like Moses, a leader must be willing to jump into the fray without having a complete knowledge of what will be required of him. A leader seizes the moment and throws himself into the middle of a conflict or crisis because desire for growth summons him to create change. He may be wrong and even downright foolish, but he is compelled to speak, choose, and act.

We may not think of ourselves as leaders, but the moment we are called to influence a person or process in a moment of chaos, we lead. We lead through an act of courage that connects us to others and to God. Every leader builds bridges of connection and tends to the fissures that threaten to divide people.

This work of connecting is a priestly dimension of leadership. It involves bridging broken parts in an attempt to reconcile those who are separated. The divide might separate two warring parties or two opposing ideas. Either way, a leader connects. He draws people to himself (connection 1) in order to take people out of a spiral that would end in chaos or destruction. Then in his attempt to forge a connection between the opposing sides (connection 2), he often draws fire from both.

More is required than merely saying, "Why can't we just get along?" More is required than wishful thinking or urging others to stop acting out of hostility. Leadership requires stepping into the morass of hurt, accusation, and defenses in order to hear and see the real issues. This ability is often described as emotional intelligence, but in fact it is wisdom tempered with the same bravado as that of the paratrooper who jumps out of an airplane into enemy territory while being strafed with machine-gun fire.

A priestly leader connects people with the vision their hearts have been warmed to pursue by reminding them of where they have come from, how they arrived here, and who they have become in the process. A priest is a community's memory and its conscience. She tells the story of its birth and the noble calling it has been written to reveal. She teaches the stories of identity: You are a child of the King. You are an heir of God. Now live in the light of your calling.

A priest must struggle with the temptation to please people rather than call them to maturity. It is far easier to tell happy stories that are full of delusions and lies than to name the story of our deceit and flight.[5]

When the new semester began at Mars Hill Graduate School after the professor had departed, Paul Steinke addressed the situation as he led our new-student orientation. It was a delicate situation in that some students didn't know or care, while other students had heard rumors and were questioning their decision to attend Mars Hill. Paul talked about both heartache and hope. He told about his concerns and how he had seen the faculty move into tough conversations yet treat one another with tender care. He acknowledged our need for grace, forgiveness, and courage, and then he boldly said, "If you want to learn how to live well in the midst of struggle and chaos rather than just reading about it, then you've come to the right place." His honesty and hope were priestly and contagious, and the semester began with a new energy.

LEADING BIRTHS NEW WAYS OF CREATING

When we normally think of a senior pastor, corporate CEO, or university president, we think of the top decision maker who hears multiple perspectives, weighs the data, and makes the final decision. He sits at the top of the pyramid, the place where the buck stops. To most people, that's what it means to be a leader.

Consider that Paul was the apostle to the Gentiles. Moses was the head of the nation of Israel. Paul Steinke was president of the student council. The leader's title usually tells the story. But in God's economy, to be king means to be a servant-shepherd. The terms *king* and *shepherd* were almost interchangeable in the ancient Near East. To be a king meant to shepherd one's people from death to life. This leader had to be vigilant, equally detail oriented and able to see the big picture. This shepherd also protected the sheep from enemies and provided them with food, water, and rest.

Many a king misunderstands or abuses his calling and ends up devouring the flock—and then he blames the sheep for the dwindling numbers. Such a leader solidifies his power by the use of fear and shame. The troops cower and obey, but they do not love the leader and they are not loyal to him. It is far more difficult to be a shepherd-king, one who must possess power and give it away until he serves as the balancing point of an inverted pyramid.

The complexity of this type of leadership required Moses to set up a hierarchy of leaders who dealt with the people in groups of thousands, hundreds, fifties, and tens.[6] This approach didn't arise from Moses' innate wisdom but from the counsel of his father-in-law, Jethro. As a leader, the king must be open to the wisdom of others and then give power to others to carry out the project.

But as *the* leader, Moses was the one about whom the people complained and the one who was attacked at each calamity. The cry was searing: "Why did you take us out of Egypt to kill us?" The words stung because they hit on his deepest doubts and fear. Every leader will feel the knife blows of betrayal and accusation from the rabble as well as from his dearest comrades. Followers enjoy nothing more than putting a leader on a throne and then waiting for him to tumble.

And since the weight of complexity and demand is so great, a leader will at some point misuse the power of his position. In Moses' fury, for instance, he struck at the rock and was forbidden to enter the Promised Land. Moses sinned and failed to enter into rest. The apostle Peter, a major leader for the Jerusalem church, had to be rebuked so as not to confuse the gospel with keeping the law of circumcision. The apostle Paul, on the other hand, didn't misuse his power, yet he ended his earthly life cold, with few friends, and begging a fellow traveler to bring him a cloak and some parchments. Failure and loss as a leader are as inevitable as the rising and setting of the sun.

The leader will fail, so he needs to confess his anger, self-absorption, and cowardice and serve his people by being the first one who needs to be forgiven. The true king takes the servant's towel and washes the feet of the strangers who are guests in his home. Not only is he the host, but he also lowers himself to the place of a bondservant in order to follow the great King who has already washed his feet and forgiven him.

As leaders, we are called to be prophets who arouse desire, priests who connect people to one another and to God, and kings who protect and provide for their people. But at the same time all of us leaders are false prophets, fake priests, and sham kings who need new desire, reconciliation, and courage. Oddly, it is in leading others to truth that we find our souls more whole-heartedly wanting what we offer to others and what we can find only in the perfect Prophet, Priest, and King: Jesus.

FACING CRISIS

The Other Shoe Weighs a Ton

I was sitting on the couch when I listened to the voice mail. As the message echoed in my head, I put the phone down and slid from a sitting position to lying down. Then I pulled a comforter up to cover my face. My wife saw me and asked what any reasonable human would ask, "What's wrong? Have you lost your mind?"

I didn't want to answer her question, and I didn't want to repeat what I had just heard on the voice mail. If I kept my head covered and my eyes closed, I could alternate between not thinking and then hyperfocusing on the quickest solution to the crisis that had just burst into my life. In a matter of seconds, however, I realized I could not hide. And there was no way to muscle through the problem to get a quick resolution.

The voice mail had informed me that the state Department of Education had decided that our vice president of academic affairs, who didn't have a doctorate or a master's degree or any past experience as an educator, was not adequate to lead our young institution. We were given just nine days to find a replacement with a PhD or we would lose our state authorization.

No member of our full-time faculty who had a doctorate wanted the position. Yet it had to be filled, and it was obvious that a slow, reasoned search could not be done in nine days. Crisis has a way of sneaking up and biting you from behind. It exposes either your lack of preparation or the foolishness of your presumption of security.

I started asking what had caused the crisis to occur at this moment, as if I could ferret out either the mind of God or the State of Washington's Department of Education. I oscillated between blaming myself for not having seen the school's vulnerability to railing against the injustice that we were given only nine days to rectify the problem.

A crisis opens up the fault lines of shame and blame. Who's at fault? Who failed to anticipate the problem? Who failed to handle the initial stages of the crisis well? In the aftermath of Hurricane Katrina in 2005, we all witnessed the aftershocks of the blame game. The city government of New Orleans was accused of failing to execute its disaster plan. The state government got a failing grade for not supporting the local government with assistance and resources. The federal government was charged with being slow and inconsistent in providing aid. Every governmental representative accused the other of indifference or worse, but initially no one took responsibility for any failure. The greater the crisis, the more we want to find someone to blame. But blame, when it is made public, only magnifies shame, which drains energy and creativity away from solving the problem.

COURAGE VERSUS BLAME

The English word *crisis* originates from the Greek *krisis,* which means "to sift or separate." Crises stir things up and divide the wheat from the chaff. As dividing moments, they force leaders to make a choice—either to risk and suffer with courage or to crumble under the weight of fear and threatening circumstances.

A crisis involves two major elements: danger and shame. Those characteristics help leaders make a distinction between an actual crisis and a "normal" problem. Consider the effect on a community when it learns that a hurricane might make landfall in less than twenty-four hours. Normal routines screech to a halt so attention and resources can be focused on preparing for the impending crisis. It is not much different when one learns that her parent has had a heart attack. In every life and in every organization, there are seasons of death, divorce, lawsuits, negative press, harassment charges, financial downturns, and staff conflict—crises that threaten our viability and integrity.

The moment a crisis exposes our perceived or actual incompetence, there will be a sense of fear and the prospect of being found out. We all feel to some degree like a poseur. We know we don't know what others presume we know. We simply are not as wise, courageous, and gifted as we want others to think, nor as much as others might presume. When a person feels exposed and found out, the natural experience is shame.

A crisis is more than a mere threat; it presents the danger of ruin. The threat of a windstorm that might bring a tree down or impede travel for a few hours is not a crisis. But a hurricane that might flatten neighborhoods and kill residents is a crisis that can bring total ruin. And compounding the danger is the shame that often follows crisis. This is how one pastor recounted his experience with crisis and shame:

> I led my first congregation through a building program, and after the building was completed, I realized that we were in debt up to our eyeballs and that we faced a major budget shortage. I feared bills not being paid and ministry not being carried out. I worked with our district to cover some of the financial expenses, but I eventually had to leave because I didn't have the training or the skill to lead the congregation through the financial mess I had created. I left this church with a feeling of failure.[1]

This pastor has gone on to serve many years in another church, but he never would have done so if he had hidden from the heartache of his earlier failure. He chose to interact with a mentor and a good counselor, and he processed the events and his own story deeply enough to be prepared for the crises that would eventually come in his future leadership positions.

But many leaders fail to take responsibility for their part in crisis and failure. In these people, failure exposes their proclivity to assign blame rather than to embrace what they can learn from the crisis. When a crisis occurs due to a leader's shortsightedness or incompetence, that blame game escalates and increases the potential for ruin.

Consider the crisis that arises when a disgruntled employee threatens to file a lawsuit against your organization. If that employee remains in his job, he might fill an important position—but he'll do so without sufficient accountability. Because of the threatened legal action, his supervisor will most likely back off from the necessary oversight of the employee's work. So who will take charge of resolving the problem? How will fear of the destructive potential of a lawsuit affect the leader of that organization? And how will the leader manage office morale and staff work load?

Often the initial crisis stirs up a swirl of debris that creates additional crises. It is similar to a hurricane spawning floods, tornadoes, and other disasters. The organization's fissures, which in the past had escaped notice, now become gaping chasms. The natural response is to blame—to take cover even at the expense of others—in order to escape shame.

Shame strips away your confidence and shatters the value that others have placed on you. Most leaders will do anything to escape a situation that could mark them with shame. People will often set up someone as the sacrificial lamb in order to deflect the shame from themselves. Crises force an organization not only to deal with the precipitating event but also to manage the natural tendency of people to hide, blame, and cover their tracks. This is one youth pastor's experience:

> The senior pastor told me prior to my coming that he…planned on
> staying for another two or three years. But he left nine months later.
> There was a group that loved him and hated to see him go. After he
> left, the anger they experienced during the grieving process was turned
> on me. I did not have the experience or insight to realize how much
> trouble was brewing until it was too late. I was treated as though I had
> committed sexual abuse. The issues were really about my organizational
> and leadership styles, and there were strong disagreements between me
> and the church leadership about how much work I should be doing.

Finally I just refused to give in to the demands…and the relationship and ministry broke apart after a year and a half. I discovered later that the senior pastor was remotely pastoring those who were directing their anger at me. It took me six months to find another church. To say this was painful is an understatment, but I realize that God had things to teach me that seminary never did. And the only way to learn was to go through that experience. I have stayed in ministry and have been in my current charge for six-and-a-half years. God used my earlier experience to prepare me.

This young man got hit by friendly fire. The crises that arise due to staff conflict, gossip, and behind-the-scenes political manuevering are legion. If the community of God refused to gossip, most crises either would not start or would not last due to the absence of fuel. Sadly, this is as likely as eradicating cancer, gout, and male-pattern baldness all on the same day.

Gossip is not merely passing on information; instead, it is the furthering of accusation and blame under the guise of relaying data. The dark underbelly of most crises is blame fueled by gossip. It causes such damage because, rather than responding to the fire that is burning, the organization has to devote personnel and resources either to putting out smaller fires or to handling false alarms.

Interestingly, the Chinese symbol for *crisis* is the merging of two signs, one meaning "danger" and the other meaning "opportunity." A crisis has the potential to transform or destroy. And what is the tipping point toward transformation in the face of crisis? The choice is either to cower in fear or to step forward with courage. The tipping point is brokenness rather than control.

CONTROL: THE CHARACTER FLAW OF COWARDICE

Crises generate a desperate need to gain control of the situation. As the threat becomes more severe, we clamor for resolution. We expect the true leader to subdue the danger with cool, calculated strength. We all want a leader who will take charge and make the crisis go away.

I have sailed in racing regattas with skippers who command the helm with an imperial authority that would make Captain Bligh cringe. Orders are bellowed. Mistakes made by a crewmember are met with withering contempt. These captains maintain despotic control through intimidation and shame.

One need only attend a kids' soccer match or, worse, a Little League baseball game to see the modus operandi of a controlling leader. He shouts at the kids, telling them where to stand and what to do. When a kid comes off the field, the coach yells, "We've gone through that drill a hundred times. What are you thinking about out there? Get your head in the game." A young player's natural response is to cringe and submit. A parent's typical response is to look away and pretend the dressing-down isn't really happening. Inside, however, most parents are wishing they could take a swing at the coach. But a bullying leader tends to silence all opposition. Would-be critics fear the confrontation that would arise if they were to question the controlling leader.

A leader whose power comes from control invariably uses his authority to punish failure. Staff members expend enormous effort to avoid a confrontation. They are overly cautious and do their job only to the measure required. A controlling leader always gets what he deserves—the bare minimum and conformity without creativity.

This response is especially true in a crisis. To effectively address a crisis, a leader must draw on creativity, intuition, wisdom, freedom, commitment, and passion. The leader who rules with intimidation squashes that kind of maneuverability and receives in its place rote, somewhat robotic, responses from his minions.

It is common, therefore, for a controlling leader to attempt to silence others and avoid personal blame by shaming others. Some leaders load on the blame without even raising their voices. Rather than shout and shame, they simply hire and retain people who know enough not to question or contradict the all-powerful Oz. You know you are with a controlling leader when there is really only one way to do things, and it is both futile and dangerous to propose a different approach.

The controlling leader must eventually become a micromanager. The devil, in this case, is truly in the details. A controlling leader doesn't trust her staff to do what needs to be done; therefore, she must dip deeper into the minutiae of the crisis. The more detail oriented she becomes, the more compulsive her actions and the narrower her view of the problem. She will get lost in the forest and not see the path, not to mention the trees.

What drives a controlling leader? Inevitably it is fear and the pursuit of power. The more control a person gains over personnel and problems, the greater his sense of mastery. The real goal of control is to eliminate chaos and uncertainty. But underneath all efforts to control is a reservoir of fear, and power is an antidote for fear. It keeps the reservoir of fear from reaching flood level. Power also freezes the top layer of fear and turns it into the ice of arrogance. The controlling leader will appear far more confident and self-assured than what is actually the case. Underneath the facade the controlling leader is terrified. He uses intimidation and shame to silence any who might get near enough to the curtain to see that the mighty Wizard of Oz is nothing more than a middle-aged man who isn't quite sure how he got there.

Here's the tragedy: power and control are a high-flying trapeze that takes a leader farther and farther above the ground with each swing. The greater his achievements, the harder it is to let go. But a leader gains true confidence only if he forces himself to let go. And confidence in the goodness of God is what a leader really needs, much more than he needs any false sense of control. But a leader will trust in the goodness of God only to the degree that he has a history of brokenness and surrender.

BROKENNESS: THE TIPPING POINT TO COURAGE

No one is humble by nature. In fact, the person who appears naturally humble is usually too lazy to be ambitious or too fearful to take risks. If a person is not tempted to control, especially in a crisis, this is often a symptom of despair and fatalism. Humility comes from humiliation, not from the choice to be self-effacing or a strong urge to give others the credit.

Humility that has not come from suffering due to one's own arrogance is either a pragmatic strategy to get along with others or a natural predilection that seems to befit only a few rare individuals. For most leaders, humility comes only by wounds suffered from foolish falls.

This is the terrible secret about leadership and life: we achieve brokenness by falling off our throne. To be broken is not a choice; it is a gift. I don't know anyone who has made the decision to be broken and achieved it as an act of the will. But to experience brokenness and humiliation, all you have to do is lead. We who lead know that things happen that make little sense and that seem to have no immediate solution yet involve some failure on our part. Listen to a leader who understands this dynamic:

> When I started in my present ministry, one of the associate pastors resigned in response to some changes I had made. He misunderstood the situation and thought I didn't want him here. He refused to believe me when I told him I wanted him to stay. He resigned without even saying good-bye to the congregation. Since he was well loved and respected, I thought this could cause dangerous reactions in the church. After talking to the board, I decided to be up-front with the congregation and tell them all the pertinent information, including the mistakes I made in the process. I learned to make decisions in prayer and to be completely honest about my most intimate motivations. This permitted me to be absolutely transparent when the situation worsened. I also learned to be honest and transparent with the flock and not hide my mistakes. The result: everybody seemed to be satisfied with the explanations and grateful for my honesty.

Leading others gives you the opportunity to first be caught in the crossfire of competing goals and agendas and then to deal with that crossfire with limited resources and inadequate information. Every decision you make in such adverse circumstances will be favored by some and opposed by others. And in such circumstances, someone will certainly consider you a failure. Leading invites humiliation and brokenness.

Clearly there are only three possible responses to the absurdity of leadership: control, flight, or brokenness. Given the futility of control and the uselessness of flight, the only viable option for leaders who want to mature is to embrace being broken.

THE ECONOMY OF BROKENNESS

Limping leaders embrace their position in God's wild economy of crisis ownership. But when crisis strikes, most of us assume we are the victims. *The crisis arose from an external source,* we reason, *and as such it is not my fault.* Since we did nothing to cause the crisis, we are only responsible to resolve it. That reaction—while common—is a recipe for disaster.

What we fail to take into account is that every crisis—even one brought on by a natural disaster—still involves people. Keeping that truth in mind, a broken leader makes this radical assumption: *The crisis is not just external; it is also internal, and it is an opportunity for me to address the failure of love in my life, whether that failure is directly or only indirectly related to the crisis.* Every crisis has the effect of revealing something about the leader's character and inner life. And often we see other people's character more clearly than our own. In the gospel of Matthew we read these words of Jesus:

> And why worry about a speck in your friend's eye when you have a log
> in your own? How can you think of saying, "Let me help you get rid of
> that speck in your eye," when you can't see past the log in your own eye?
> Hypocrite! First get rid of the log from your own eye; then perhaps you
> will see well enough to deal with the speck in your friend's eye.[2]

Acknowledging and dealing with the logs in our own eyes is a step toward humility, toward being broken by the truth about ourselves. To be broken embraces four realities:

1. *I am never sufficiently good, wise, or gifted to make things work.*

2. *My failures will harm others, the process, and myself, no matter how hard I try to avoid failure.*

3. *The greatest harm I can do is to try to limit the damage I cause by not participating, by quitting, or by pushing for control.*

4. *Calling out for help from God and others is the deepest confession of humility.*

To be humiliated—that is, to publicly fall off our throne of power—is to stand face to face with the deepest and truest reality of life: We were never meant to have God's power. We are not God.

I can't make my organization thrive. I can't make my daughter believe. I can't create intimate joy with my wife. I have very little control even over my own thoughts, feelings, and choices. Oh, I have some, but it is naive and arrogant to assume I have full dominion over myself so that I can do whatever I choose.

What I do have the power to do is to enter the flow of paradox. There's a very good reason why confessing one's failure to have control is the first step in the redemptive Alcoholics Anonymous process. With that confession we embrace our brokenness and let go of the futile effort to manage our addiction—whatever it might be.

No leaders can avoid crises, and every crisis demands the best of a leader's energy. But the more effort leaders expend trying to be in control, the less energy they have available to respond to the crisis. It is the difference between oak and bamboo. An oak is a strong, proud tree; bamboo is a grass. An oak, in its regal inflexibility, stands against rain and wind until the wind is too great, and then its inflexibility makes it more susceptible to breaking. Bamboo, however, will bend with the wind and is flexible enough not to break. That oak-bamboo contrast illustrates what may be one of the strangest dimensions of being a broken leader: our brokenness results not in being crushed but in the capacity to flex and change rather than to remain brittle and vulnerable.

Lee, the leader of an emerging church, is bamboo, but he didn't begin that way. He writes,

A year ago we faced a situation where up to one-half of our church community was going to be leaving us in the span of three months. They were moving on to new jobs or grad school, or they were leaving due to graduation. Not only were we losing a significant percentage of our church membership, but the people who were moving represented leadership in almost every area of our community as well as a large percentage of our financial base. We faced the very real possibility of having to shut down simply for lack of people to carry out what needed to be accomplished. My first response was to curl up in a fetal position in the corner and wait for the end.

A broken leader is no longer driven by the need to impress people or to secure their approval. A broken leader has already known shame, so there is little fear of being found out or further exposed as a failure. This is not to say she doesn't care what others think or is so self-sufficient that praise and delight are beneath her. As I'll explain in a moment, the opinions of others are, for a broken leader, both data and delight. But she doesn't live and die by the way others judge her.

Regarding data and delight, I see strong disapproval as simply additional data to consider in the process of understanding both yourself and the path you have chosen. Strong approval is a delight and is a humbling reminder that even a blind squirrel occasionally bumps into an acorn. When a broken leader's labor is blessed, it is a significant reminder that success is neither earned by hard work nor a reward for faithfulness. Instead, success is a token of grace to be enjoyed in the moment before the other shoe drops.

So why do we fear the fall of the other shoe? The artillery shell might land directly on the foxhole that you dug with your bare hands out of the frozen earth. That is unfair, but it also is reality. A broken leader is not afraid to die, because he holds few, if any, illusions about life. He knows that accolades today will be the basis of deeper disappointment when those who laud don't get their way in the next bout of decisions. A broken leader holds to fewer and fewer illusions about life; he doesn't hold to life as anything other than a passing gift—undeserved, unbidden, and glorious. The more we are freed by the love of God from the tentacles of shame and blame, the less likely we will be to give in to fear during a crisis. It is brokenness that increases a heart's capacity to live with courage.

What is courage? G. K. Chesterton wrote,

> Courage is almost a contradiction in terms. It means a strong desire to
> live taking the form of a readiness to die. "He that will lose his life, the
> same shall save it," is not a piece of mysticism for saints and heroes....
> A soldier surrounded by enemies, if he is to cut his way out, needs to
> combine a strong desire for living with a strange carelessness about
> dying. He must not merely cling to life, for then he will be a coward,
> and will not escape. He must not merely wait for death, for then he
> will be a suicide, and will not escape. He must seek his life in a spirit
> of furious indifference to it; he must desire life like water, and yet drink
> death like wine.[3]

The essence of courage is not an absence of fear; it is the necessary paradox of leadership. Facing the extremity of our helplessness opens the door to the freedom to fight with a "strange carelessness" and a "spirit of furious indifference." This is the foundation for true confidence.

CONFIDENCE: EMBRACING THE GOOD STORY

If confidence is nothing more than the assurance that we are right, then confidence is nothing more than well-groomed arrogance. True confidence is courage that has been humbled. A limping leader understands this: *I don't know if I am right, nor am I sure the path chosen is the best, but after reflection, feedback, debate, and prayer, I am choosing this path. In the process, I will seek life like water and drink death like wine.*

A confident leader remembers her own story of redemption. She remembers that in the past God has been good to give her favor and a way out of disaster; therefore, she borrows lessons from the past to invest in the crisis du jour. She is sure of past redemption and gambles that in some fashion and time, good will be mined from the current disaster—even if the results of the crisis flow contrary to her desire. This confidence is reflected in Paul's view of death in the book of Philippians. He wrote,

> For to me, to live is Christ and to die is gain. If I am to go on living in
> the body, this will mean fruitful labor for me. Yet what shall I choose?
> I do not know! I am torn between the two: I desire to depart and be
> with Christ, which is better by far; but it is more necessary for you that
> I remain in the body. Convinced of this, I know that I will remain, and
> I will continue with all of you for your progress and joy in the faith,
> so that through my being with you again your joy in Christ Jesus will
> overflow on account of me.[4]

What if I make a huge mistake and get fired? What if I am hated because of the decision I'm about to make? What if the current crisis takes the organization down? These are not small matters, nor are they to be addressed in a cavalier manner. But what is the worst that can occur? Public exposure and shame? Loss of reputation? Harsh judgment from those I have failed? None of these experiences is easy, but they are not equivalent to death. They may be humiliating, but they don't require the loss of our hearts and souls. If death is not my ultimate foe, then anything less than death is truly a small enemy. And it's not an enemy that has the power to rob me of worth or of joy.

A broken leader is a sweet paradox of confidence and openness. If those I lead have already found out the worst there is to know about me—that I am a sinner—then the log in my eye is continually being removed in the midst of every crisis. The result is better vision and greater wisdom due to the freedom I feel to both live and die.

Lee, the pastor I mentioned earlier whose church was losing one-half of its congregation, went on to say this:

My first response was to curl up in a fetal position in the corner and wait for the end. Realizing the lack of usefulness in such a response, I spent some time evaluating several factors: (1) I thought about what God has called me to be as a leader and what God has called our community to be. I recognized that neither of those had changed, and therefore, something must be coming that would answer all of the needs that would arise with the impending exodus. (2) I spent a lot of time thinking about, reading about, and remembering the ability of God as he has demonstrated it through the Bible and through the story of our community. (3) I started to look around at who would be left and realized how God was preparing us for what was to come. People who had not been in leadership were hanging out with and learning from those who were. Consequently the troops rallied to our call as a community and to the possibilities of life beyond the leavings.

We saw people step into roles that we had never pegged them for and watched them flourish. Our community became more organic as old things were dropped and new things begun. Losing friends was painful, and some of the adjustments are still not what we would like them to be, but all in all this experience was a good thing for our church and for me. I don't know how much courage was involved. I think I would call it confidence in who God is and faith reinforced by remembering what he had done and what he had promised. Maybe that's a definition of courage. I do know that I was scared to fail, scared to lose what we had worked so hard for, scared to have to figure out what to do next. So much of the male identity is tied to what we do, and I was afraid of losing a lot of that in losing the church. On the other side, though, I'm finding myself more confident in who I am as a leader and in the people who are a part of our community. Moving forward into uncertainty has become much easier. I wouldn't choose to go through this season again, but I feel like I would be able to weather it. I also know better how to approach another crisis that comes.

Lee wanted to curl up in a fetal position and hide. What leader has not felt that strong desire to escape? Yet Lee came to his senses and remembered his calling. He recalled the stories that our faith is grounded on, and he began to plan. He walked into the chaos and called others to do the same, and his community came alive.

Lee's broken courage didn't seem courageous to him. Courage never does to the person exercising it. Besides, nearly every hero reports: "I couldn't have done anything other than what I did." Courage never takes away fear; courage simply redistributes fear to get the job done. As Anne Lamott said in a public lecture, "Courage is fear that has said its prayers."[5]

The great gain for the organization will be a leader who knows that the more control he exerts in the face of crisis, the more out of control he will be. On the other hand, the greater his embrace of the paradox of brokenness, the more courage he will gain for facing the threat of danger. Leading with a limp works by inversion and paradox. You are the strongest when you are weak, and you are the most courageous when you are broken.

You find your greatest effectiveness as a leader when you lead with a distinct limp.

RESPONDING TO THE FIVE LEADERSHIP CHALLENGES

In this chapter I have presented cowardice as the ineffective default response to crisis. Facing the dangers inherent in any crisis, a leader typically seeks to control people and circumstances in order to avoid blame and shame. He lacks the courage to weather the potential damage to his reputation.

Crisis is only the first of the five inevitable challenges of leadership, and cowardice is the natural—and ineffective—response that I have observed most often in myself and in many other leaders. But each leader is different, and in your work you might find that you tend to meet crises with narcissism or possibly rigidity, rather than cowardice.

Look again at the first chart on page 8 in the introduction. It identifies a common and ineffective response to each of the five challenges of leadership. In the interest of bringing some clarity to these five challenges, I've linked the issue of crisis with the ineffective response of cowardice, the issue of complexity with rigidity, the issue of betrayal with narcissism, the issue of loneliness with hiding, and the issue of weariness with fatalism. Each response is natural, but each one will render you ineffective as a leader because with none of these responses do you draw strength from your leader's limp.

Granted, each person and context is different, so the default reactions to leadership challenges vary from one leader to the next and from one circumstance to the next. What the following chapters provide is a matrix of relationships that heuristically will invite you to consider your own responses to the biggest challenges of leadership. Individually, the next four chapters take a closer look at complexity, betrayal, loneliness, and weariness, and a leader's typical failed responses to each of these challenges. At the same time we will look at the inverted effectiveness of such limping responses as depth in the face of complexity, gratitude in response to betrayal, openness that overcomes loneliness, and hope to combat weariness.

6

THE PROBLEM OF COMPLEXITY

All Leaders See Through a Glass Darkly

It is always a mistake to look at your e-mail before having your second cup of coffee in the morning. I know this to be true, yet I seldom do what I know is best. If I did, I would eat oatmeal instead of Frosted Flakes. I'd exercise, set a time for quiet, and not turn on the *Today* show to see what Katie Couric is wearing.

E-mail is the great scourge of modern communication. It facilitates the passing on of simple information, yet it forces complex matters to be presented in a fashion that makes what is difficult appear easy and, in many cases, what is peripheral seem central. E-mail distorts. It allows thoughtful and reasonable communication to appear deranged and fury laden. And if you read e-mail with only half of your synapses firing, you are doomed. Coffee helps, but e-mail still adds to the darkness of the looking glass.

At no time in the history of humanity has more information been available at our fingertips, and most of it is useless. I decided a few seconds ago to Google the phrase *Tibetan sexual mores*. Within .32 seconds I had 3,450 sites to consider. The Internet is a blessing; it is a curse. If I really did want to know about Buddhist sexual philosophy, how could I know which of these thousands of sources is authoritative?

So you and I are stranded in the information highway's vast traffic jam, saturated with unusable information. And as big an issue as this complex information boom is, it still is the least significant factor of our seeing through a dark glass. The far greater complexity of life is the result of sin. The heart is said to be too convoluted to know. We don't fully understand our own motivation, let alone the heart of another. We can never be perfectly clear about the matters that are most important to us, so we stumble along with hopes that over time some of the dust will settle and we'll be able to see a little more clearly. We ought to take comfort, however, that even after the Resurrection and Jesus' return to teach his disciples the meaning of what had occurred, the Eleven were still confused about what it all meant. God's plan becomes completely clear only from the vantage point of heaven.

NOT ALL COMPLEXITY IS COMPLEX

Sometimes leaders allow apparent complexity to obscure what is in fact a rather simple, but admittedly difficult, decision. Years ago, for instance, our executive team struggled with a hire that had been made without sufficient due diligence. The need to fill the open slot had been great, and there had been few applicants. The person who hired the new staff member was inexperienced and felt pressure from others to fill the position quickly.

The new hire was not a good fit, and everyone knew it from the first day when she stayed in her office in an almost catatonic state. Efforts to draw her out were met with polite distance and a closed door. We kept her in her job for nearly a month. It was miserable for her as well as for those with whom she worked.

The only humane and wise choice would have been to let her go as soon as possible. But we didn't because there seemed to be so many competing and complex issues. She was a dear friend of someone who worked with us. She had received great reviews from her previous supervisor. So we thought perhaps she would adjust. We desperately needed the job filled, and to begin a new search seemed overwhelming in light of the fact that no better candidates had applied. No one wanted to admit that a mistake had been made, no one had a better idea about what to do next, and we were concerned that staff morale would plummet if we fired our new hire. We had many factors to consider, but the decision itself was simple: she needed to go.

Now, when I work with clients in therapy, I often hear the phrase "I don't know" when the person really means "I don't *want* to know." Likewise, if a situation is sufficiently complex, we leaders often feel that the difficulty of the matter lets us off the hook and gives us permission not to know and, therefore, not to act.

Choosing confusion over action can be a ruse to escape hard but simple decisions. It is always wise to ask yourself, *Do I know what to do but simply not want to do it?* That's understandable because even simple decisions are daunting when they bear the weight of looming uncertainty as to what will happen next.

LOOKING THROUGH THE THICK PART OF THE GLASS

Beyond the simple decisions that we often put off or avoid altogether are the truly complex circumstances that arise in any organization or ministry. And a situation or decision becomes complex any time that past, present, and future collide.

The Past: Competing Grids

Every one of us interprets data from an existing schema. For example, as I wrote this at almost four o'clock in the afternoon, I heard someone enter the house. This was the time my son usually got home from high school. The front door opened with an adolescent force, and I shouted, "Andrew?" My wife answered, and though her voice was calm, I knew something had upset her because she doesn't normally open the door with such intensity. I expected my son, but in fact it was my wife. We always predict the future by reading the present from a frame of reference that was established in the past. In this case I was wrong about my son's arriving home, but with the new data in hand, I accurately concluded that something was troubling my wife.

Complexity arises when the grids we use to interpret the present seem to be breaking down or when another grid competes for ascendancy. This is one of the most common causes of complexity in the church. Consider when a member of the pastoral staff may need to be fired but also redeemed. We often feel bound to keep someone in a position that isn't a good fit, when in the business world that person would have been sent packing in a heartbeat. But in the church we continue to "work" with him because redemption is viewed as more important in many circles than competence; and even more so, redemption is often defined as keeping a person in a job they aren't doing well until they dissolve or quit under the pressure. For some reason, though, we refuse to see that redemption can be advanced by dismissing an employee who is ill suited for his position.

As you read this, you can hear the various objections to ending his employment: "But I thought you were committed to relationships" or "I thought we were like a family." One church planter had operated according to the core schema that relationships are primary, but then he found himself facing a situation in which a long-held friendship conflicted with the pastoral needs of his congregation:

> I had planted a church with my best friend. About nine months after
> we launched it, I discovered that he was really struggling to do his job.
> Eventually I realized that I needed to ask him to step down. It was the
> hardest thing I've ever had to do. My greatest fear was losing his friend-
> ship. I did not want to confront him, but I knew I needed to for the
> sake of the church. I had to seriously wrestle with whether or not the
> church was worth losing a twelve-year friendship over.
>
> I remember meeting him at a restaurant. I was shaking and ner-
> vous when I confronted him. I had written an outline of the things I
> needed to say. I took a deep breath, prayed, and went for it. The con-
> versation was tough, but it went rather well. I gave him two weeks to
> consider whether or not he could do the job. By the time the two

weeks were up, he realized that the job was over his head. The crisis, though, shook my confidence. This happened two years ago, and I still feel confused by the event. He left the church, which crushed me. This has also impacted my theology. Is the church really worth such relational fallout? If the church is really about spiritual relationships, then why are they so hard to keep together?

When a way of thinking about life begins to break down or compete with another way of seeing reality, we will experience a period of overwhelming complexity. It is, therefore, imperative to constantly ask, *What lens am I using to read reality?*

The Present: Ambiguity

The lens I use comes from a grid that was formed in the past, but I use it to "see" in the present. Seeing is not a passive act: the grid that was formed in the past plays an active role in shaping what we see in the present and how we see it. We see what our grid has predisposed us to see. For example, a middle-aged male staying at a nice hotel gets on an elevator at the eighth floor to go to the lobby. He doesn't "see" the same thing that a young woman sees when she enters the elevator at the seventh floor. He may barely notice who is on the elevator; she invariably will notice, and she will find a space that feels the safest from prying eyes or groping hands. The man never gives a thought to his personal safety; the woman sees safety as foremost.

Keeping that illustration in mind, we must humble ourselves and ask questions that often go unaddressed: *What am I not seeing in this situation? What grid am I imposing on my world that keeps me from seeing more fully? What bias from my ethnic, socioeconomic, religious, national, or experiential grids is blinding me to my situation?* The questions may not immediately open the door to a new way of seeing, but the effort will remind us that how we typically see a person or situation is likely not the whole truth. Our grid compels us to see certain data as primary and other things as less important. We are always gambling that we see enough to get a true view of reality—and we usually lose. We don't see all that is present, and what we do see is often distorted by the bias of our operating grid. If it weren't, we would be omniscient.

Add to all of this the really big issue: we hate ambiguity. Data that competes with and contradicts how we saw the problem an hour ago befuddles and annoys us. We don't want to give up our favorite stereotypes, principles, convictions—because we would then be forced to say, "It could be this, or that, or something I've not yet named." One leader confesses that he welcomes new data only when it provides a way out of the mess:

> Often I try to deal with the complexity with simplicity because I get
> weary of tension. I don't like ambiguity. I know it's part of the reality
> of life, but I still don't like it. When I feel out of control, I pray that I'll
> hit my knees and surrender to the One who lacks no clarity. I'm willing
> to think outside the box or hear ideas like this if they make sense of the
> complexity or at least help me manage it.

When we hate ambiguity, we will often choose a solution that may seem right, but it may simply perpetuate the status quo. Also, if we demand that any new way of thinking reduces the "work" of leading (simplifying), we will fail to enter the chaos and try to see through a new lens. When we pray simply for resolution, we cheat ourselves out of the opportunity to grow. Finding the grid that we need—if we hope to make the best decisions and move our organizations into the future—will necessarily invite us to enter the chaos and live with the uncertainty.

The Future: Uncertainty

We hate ambiguity because we hate feeling out of control. If we knew with certainty that what we were doing was "right" as measured by some external standard, we could relax. We could wade into chaos and face every hard decision with confidence.

I sometimes ask leaders, "How would you feel about this situation if you knew in advance that it would not only turn out well but would one day be seen as one of your greatest accomplishments?" The answer from most people is "relief," "pride," or "joy." With prior knowledge of a positive outcome, we could enter every difficult situation with confidence. But when complex situations arise, fear and confusion keep us from anticipating a good outcome.

When the past fails to offer us a sure guide, and when the present information is incomplete, contradictory, and skewed by our biases, then the future feels violently up for grabs. It is often in this moment that we gravitate to rigidity, to a narrowing of options that pretends to simplify the complexity. We desperately want to believe the empty promise of certainty.

RIGIDITY: THE CHARACTER FLAW OF DOGMATISM

Dogmatism assures us that we know the answer before we bother to look. On the surface, this approach seems to make life simpler, but it almost always steers us in the wrong direction.

Dogmatism, after all, is not about what we believe but how we hold those beliefs. After World War II many studies were done in an attempt to understand the rise of authoritarian, despotic ideologies and governments. It was discovered that a fascist despot and a communist demagogue are more alike than different. Their beliefs are contradictory, but their personalities and ways of leading are almost identical.

Likewise, a dogmatic religious fundamentalist is more similar to a dogmatic atheist than he is to people who share his beliefs but who are still seeking greater clarity in their beliefs. The common link between contradictory ideologies is rigidity or the refusal to remain open to new beliefs and new ways of understanding old convictions.

Rigidity is a refusal to reframe; it is a kind of thinking that limits the range of options and implications. To clarify, it is not dogmatic to believe Jesus was raised bodily from the dead and that he ascended into heaven. It is dogmatic, however, to think that you already know and can limit the range of meaning implied by these beliefs. For example, in what ways does our understanding of the Incarnation directly influence how we live as middle-class consumers in the face of widespread poverty? To think we understand the meaning of the Incarnation is arrogant, let alone to think we have mined its significance for a godly engagement with life.

Consider this example of rigidity and its impact in the workplace. The following e-mail from a lay counselor who is part of a church counseling ministry describes what happens when a leader is entrenched in a solution that doesn't take into consideration other essential grids.

> Our director, Mary, is a therapist who sees a full-time load of clients, so there is little time for her to talk with us about our clients. Unfortunately, she doesn't want other professionals in the ministry, so she is our only resource for supervision and training.
>
> Four months ago in our monthly meeting, we counselors openly voiced concerns about our training and supervision. Longings were expressed for other professionals and speakers to come to our meetings to direct and counsel us. People were kind and honest in voicing what they felt was lacking. The tension was palpable, but at least we were talking instead of being nicey-nice. At one point a lay counselor asked the director if she thought she was efficient at administration. Mary heard this as an attack and defended her leadership.
>
> Long story short, the man who asked Mary the question was relieved from the ministry. Mary felt his gifts would be better utilized in a different place. She added that she had been having problems with him all along and that the firing had nothing to do with what he said in the meeting.
>
> When Mary fired this man, it became a catalyst. In our next meeting she didn't allow any time slotted to discuss issues. I got in a huff and asked Mary why we were pretending everything was fine and if we could talk together as a team. No, not enough time. We asked Mary if we could meet together on Sunday afternoon with her, and she said yes. But a few days before the meeting, Mary had her secretary call and

cancel. Then we received a letter saying that she was canceling our monthly meetings for the rest of the year and that she wanted to meet with us individually in order to build relationships with us. Elders and staff are now involved. Mary feels betrayed; feelings are hurt.

It is a tangled web. The sad thing for me is that I like Mary personally, and I know she has helped a lot of folks. I have called her and written to her. She sincerely believes that the team fell apart because the attitude of the man she fired had brought too much "negativity" to the team. As with all stories, there is so much more.

Clearly Mary is not broken by the conflict in this ministry, nor has she apparently looked deeply at the log in her own eye. But there is another problem here: she has opted for rigidity. She clamors for control by framing the problem as an issue of negativity. She has a bad apple on staff, her thinking goes, so she simply removes the apple, exposes the contamination, and rebuilds trust through interactions with individuals. Mary might be correct about the person she fired, but the problem requires a far more complex analysis than she seems willing to pursue.

Rigidity always results in an us-versus-them mentality. Wherever you see polarities—good/bad, right/wrong, left/right—you know the real issue has been oversimplified. Black-and-white dogmatism has been exercised in an attempt to avoid complexity. No issue worthy of reflection can truly be understood by reducing it to polarities. Greater depth and broader exploration are needed.

The moment a leader sees any issue or person in terms of a binary, she has embraced dogmatism and rigidity. Such a leader would do well to ask herself what she is fleeing and why she avoids the pursuit of deeper thinking.

FOOLISHNESS: THE TIPPING POINT TO DEPTH

A leader must be a fool, and a fool is someone neither bound to convention nor tied to the dictates of the powerful. A fool lives on and beyond the edge;

he is a boundary breaker. The apostle Paul spoke in favor of this kind of fool-ishness when he wrote,

> For the message of the cross is foolishness to those who are perishing,
> but to us who are being saved it is the power of God. For it is written:
> > "I will destroy the wisdom of the wise;
> > > the intelligence of the intelligent I will frustrate."...
> But God chose the foolish things of the world to shame the wise;
> God chose the weak things of the world to shame the strong. He chose
> the lowly things of this world and the despised things—and the things
> that are not—to nullify the things that are, so that no one may boast
> before him. It is because of him that you are in Christ Jesus, who has
> become for us wisdom from God—that is, our righteousness, holiness
> and redemption.[1]

God inverts expectations, paradigms, and human wisdom. He chooses the foolish and the weak to subvert our natural tendency to pride. A leader's wis-dom can't be conventional and still be fully Christian. The nature of biblical wisdom is that it can't be subsumed under any one structure, group, or denom-ination; therefore, any attempt to rigidly define and control truth is like try-ing to contain water in your hands. Truth will always resist being boxed into a tight, coherent, controllable system.

One wise leader discussed the interplay between chaos, control, and the irony of God's "foolish" way of engaging us. He wrote,

> I *know* that I possess no control over anything, and those who appear
> to possess it are paying a very high price in terms of manipulative and/or
> abusive behavior, something I simply will not get into. The control we
> crave is an illusion, and in the end even God himself doesn't always get
> his way on this planet. If he did, we wouldn't have been exhorted to
> pray "thy kingdom come, thy will be done on earth." At difficult times
> I have to exit the logical process and turn to what the Lord may drop

into my consciousness, seemingly out of nowhere. And another thing. When that happens, not infrequently it is an experience of God's ironic sense of humor.

A leader-fool is free enough to operate outside tradition and conventional wisdom, but wise enough to take advantage of any voice, no matter its source. And one of the best sources of perspective is enemies. If we can learn from them, then we can profit from anyone. Enemies mean to do us harm with biased and often cruel words. But many times the assault begins, ends, or is peppered with enough truth to make the assault credible and the wounds worthy of careful attention.

Yet we typically prefer the readily available perspective; we reach for what's on the surface rather than choosing to go deeper. Often we fail to listen to our enemies, or even to those on our side who strenuously disagree with us, because considering their words would stir up too much dust. Now, I don't recommend sitting down with your enemies as a daily habit, but on occasion you can learn much about yourself from them.

A leader-fool is unafraid of chaos or confrontation. She does not rely on the false security of rigidity. After all, the greater the ambiguity of the situation, the more likely a leader will need to surrender the tried-and-true and be open to a new and deeper way of engaging a problem. Each encounter with a different view of our situation will provide new data, clearer themes, and a greater number of paths to choose from. We gain wisdom as we open our thinking to multiple perspectives. Whether we're learning from our enemies, submitting our views to vocal critics, or relentlessly evaluating our grids, the result is greater flexibility and new ways of thinking. One leader has made this effort a formal process:

> When faced with a complex situation, I am very logical and analytical.
> I try to deconstruct the issue from both macro and micro levels. I
> think through the problem and try to identify the issue. Then I forget
> everything I have just assumed and decided about the issue and try to

approach it with a whole different set of assumptions and conclusions. By doing this multiple times, I am able to see answers and solutions that would otherwise never have been apparent.

The book of Proverbs tells us that wisdom is found in multiple counselors. Not multiple yes-men or yes-women saying relatively the same thing. In disharmony—contradictory views and opinions—a new synthesis can arise. We need chaos and disharmony if we are to see a problem, a person, or a process in a new light.

Remember the description of Mary, the leader of the lay counseling ministry? "People were kind and honest in voicing what they felt was lacking. The tension was palpable, but at least we were talking instead of being nicey-nice." The expected tension was present, but Mary dismissed the discussion that was needed in favor of individual meetings where she could try to manage the chaos and the hurt.

A leader-fool would have trod across the boundaries of propriety and the fear of hurt feelings and allowed the issues to surface. A leader-fool would have led the charge, brought the divergent views of the situation to the table, and befriended each of the perspectives in order to take in all that could be learned. A leader-fool would allow chaos to birth creativity and would open the process to all the members of the community who are invested in the decision. Listen to how one pastor approaches the task of leading through complexity:

Doing what I do know to do helps me identify the following step. It is similar to driving on a dark night with the headlights on. I can't tell you what is five hundred feet in front of me, but I can see the next two hundred feet. As I travel, I eventually see what I couldn't see before.

Issues of control also ease up as I release people into leadership and ministry. I find people who are more qualified than I, who better understand the issue at hand and the purpose of our church, and I seek their wisdom, guidance, and direction. Thinking outside of the box is best done with a balance of alone time, typically while relaxing or exercising or reading, and being open to direction. Then the solution comes. Also, gathering a group to brainstorm creatively over a number of sessions can provide steps to resolve complex issues.

CREATIVITY: OPENING YOUR HEART TO MEANING

The more complex the situation, the more we tend to resort to analysis. To analyze something means to dissect it until we come to an understanding that we believe allows us to predict, manage, and control the problem. But chaos theory reminds us that every effort to measure, let alone control, a phenomenon not only changes it but moves it in an unpredictable direction. Control is the province of idiots, not leader-fools.

So instead of analyzing it, we need to dance with the chaos. Dancing with the confounding unknown requires a conviction that deep, invisible patterns of order—patterns that are profoundly independent of our control—are to be found when we actively surrender to nuance, mystery, and surprise. If we wish to be leader-fools, we must jump deeply into the unseen and dance with the chaos until order appears.

Imagine living out the belief that creativity finds its best soil in the dirt of chaos. One pastor describes well the tension and glory of living in chaos with an open heart:

> Our desire is to be organic and creative and offer a variety in the elements of our worship, but we have some folks who come from a more music-focused tradition who want the band to be bigger and louder and more central to what we do. Others would rather we never sang, and on it goes. As a leader, my role is to find ways all these folks can experience God in worship, to maintain their sense of community with one another, and to help shape the direction of our times together. Some days it feels like I'm juggling flaming chain saws.

The reality of leadership chaos can't be better named: "juggling flaming chain saws." No wonder we'd prefer shutting the chain saw off and dousing the flames. But to do so creates the monotony and rigidity of having only one "style." While such an approach offers order, it singles out one way as inherently the best or the right way.

If we want something better than just one "right" way, we must seek the input of people who will help us find a different path from the one we would come up with on our own. Notice, however, that this is not an exercise at all in seeking consensus. We don't manage complexity by coming to the perfect and unanimously approved plan before we move forward. Many leaders want order and full agreement in order to take a risk. But true creativity requires risk as the precondition for a new harmony to rise. In the words of the pastor juggling the flaming chain saws:

> I have found that creating an environment where creativity and counterintuitive thinking is valued also allows for greater grace when things don't work as we'd hoped they would. In our experience of dealing with worship, we have weeks where things just simply do not work for anyone. When those weeks come, we acknowledge the failure and move forward. People in our community know this is a part of who we are, and it has become okay.

A leader-fool knows God's ways are not conventional or obvious. If they were, then the Old Testament law would be all we need to function well on this earth. But in God's kingdom we operate by grace, which is an inverted logic that is both rational and paradoxical.

Jazz offers a profound example of grace. Jazz musicians are not merely playing any note they wish. They do not abandon logic, structure, or rationality. The art lies in the musicians' fundamental playing skills that push them to engage not just a musical score but one another.

Strict adherence to the rules merely leads to retaining the status quo. A leader-fool knows the rules and could play the score with strict compliance if he chooses, but he realizes that most complexity will not submit to our demand for order. When we do attempt to impose order and control the situation, all we get is new disorder.

A leader-fool also knows that chaos opens the door to an opportunity to submit to a new kind of listening and receiving, a kind that requires us to know the other players—their unique skills, idiosyncrasies, weaknesses, and strengths. Then from the practice of listening and receiving, as well as from the implicit call to create from the shards of disorder, a new and deeper discovery of meaning will arise.

That discovery is always incomplete and temporary, however. It is not an answer, but it is a valuable new vantage point from which to reaffirm the core questions that an organization or ministry needs to address again and again. What most organizations want is clarity—the banishing of ambiguity and a plan that is guaranteed to work. But a limping leader who lives and breathes faith won't offer those restraints. Instead, she offers an open field on which to play and to fail, to reframe and redesign. The process of chaos-induced creativity invites us to surrender to the God who honors all creativity with new chaos and, with it, opportunities to re-create again and again. A leader-fool blesses complexity because she knows it will humble the team, expose their idols of control, and invite them both to listen with greater depth and to open their hearts to the inverted, odd, paradoxical ways of God.

7

No More Jackasses

Wrestling with Betrayal Without Becoming a Jerk

*Again I looked and saw all the oppression that was taking place
under the sun:*

I saw the tears of the oppressed—
    and they have no comforter;
power was on the side of their oppressors—
    and they have no comforter.
And I declared that the dead,
    who had already died,
are happier than the living,
    who are still alive.
But better than both
    is he who has not yet been,
who has not seen the evil
    that is done under the sun.

*And I saw that all labor and all achievement spring from man's envy
of his neighbor. This too is meaningless, a chasing after the wind.*

The book of Ecclesiastes is thick, blood-red meat to a world that prefers the more easily digested milk of simple solutions. If the writer is accurate, the motivation of most leaders is not greed or even power, but envy. It is not inaccurate to say people live for the "green," but the green is not money. It is envy.

The passage that opened this chapter suggests that envy is what breeds the oppression of the weak and that envy is the reason the oppressed have no comforters. In fact, it is better to have never been born than to have to suffer a world made mad and cruel through envy. Envy makes a human heart beastly—like an ass.

Note the difficult message being delivered to those who have power: if you exercise power and authority over others, you are probably an oppressor. We leaders misuse our power when we envy what we perceive others possess and then attempt to take it from them. Envy arises because we are not grateful for how God has written our world or for how he has blessed us. Envy comes from a sense of inadequacy and emptiness rooted in our woundedness. The more a person is driven by emptiness and inadequacy, the more self-centered and violent that person will become—and the more oppression he will bring into the world.

When leaders fail to deal with their woundedness, they fall into patterns of envy and oppression. That's why it is imperative that as leaders we look behind the curtain.

BETRAYAL: THE WOUND OF ENVY

Envy is not a fancy word for greed. People motivated by greed don't usually choose to be leaders—they rob banks. A leader is often a wounded individual who feels drawn to rectify, to amend, the suffering she has endured in the past. It sounds noble, and often is, until new wounds of betrayal are suffered that repeat the original harm. Then the nastiness begins.

A leader who has either not faced his wounds or acknowledged the defenses

he has erected as protection from harm may become cruel, defensive, belittling, arrogant, emotionally insulated, and even a sexual predator—reflecting
some of the characteristics we associate with the term *narcissism*. The more
powerful the person's leadership position, the more likely it is that the leader
has narcissistic characteristics. But it is not uncommon for the same traits to
be found in less powerful leaders or even among people who don't occupy a
formal leadership position.

Most leaders, however, do have a significant history of betrayal that motivates them to grasp the reins of leadership, and it's ironic that the role of leader
brings with it the guarantee of being betrayed. The wounds suffered in the
process of leading are so predictable as to be commonplace, yet their effect is
devastating. Read the stories that follow, tales taken from the lives of men and
women in leadership, and imagine what it would be like to endure the same
heartaches.

Toward the end of my time at the church, outright lies about me were
being told by the senior pastor, his wife, and the people they had surrounded themselves with. The wife would call me at three in the morning several nights a week, when she was awake and feeling emotionally
unstable, and scream accusations at me until I had to take the phone
off the hook.

A group of older ladies in my first church did not want a female pastor.
No matter what I did, they were not happy. I tried to listen and accom-
modate their wishes, to no avail. They personally attacked me to try to
run me out of the church.

On numerous occasions I have had complaints about my leadership.
Unfortunately, these complaints were made not to me but to others I
serve. I felt betrayed, especially because the people who had spoken out
against me were friendly and complimentary to my face. I had to hear
their negative comments from others.

I was an elected lay leader in a local church. The betrayal came from
the pastor whom I had confided in. He had used my honest confi-
dences in him about my inadequacies and failures to judge my character and to serve as evidence for why I shouldn't be in leadership.

Betrayal is a deep psychic wound that hardens the heart against grief and
deadens its hunger for intimacy. Grief is meant to open our hearts and eventually move us to receive the care of others. But what if we feel profound
shame along with our grief? Shame distances us from people and the comfort
they could offer us in our grief; shame also causes a person to hate the innate
desire to be connected with others.

Betrayal comes primarily in one of two forms: abandonment or abuse. A
father who offers to play a quick game of catch with his son or daughter but
then takes a phone call and forgets to return to the game has disappointed his
child. If that pattern happens repeatedly with no efforts on Dad's part to
rebuild the broken relationship, then his child will steel herself against more
disappointment. An absentee father creates a father-wound that bleeds deep,
and the wound is most often sutured by the victim's decision to care less. But
the less one cares, the harder the heart becomes and the more resolute that person becomes to shut out the involvement of others. Any stirring of desire for
deep connection with others will feel hopeless and pointless.

Abuse is an even worse form of betrayal. A mother who physically, sexually, or emotionally abuses her child, or who allows abuse to be perpetrated,
abandons her child. Such a mother sets the child up to desire goodness and
protection, but she gives the child a snake instead. The child's rage becomes
deeply embedded as a defense against the shame of being used and then dis-
carded. The wound is intractable but often hidden under a guise of fearlessness and independence. If a leader seeks to lead in the conventional way, then
fearlessness and independence are two of the leader's most powerful assets.

Now consider the resulting leadership trap that seems impossible to
escape: what a typical follower wants is protection from fear and freedom from
choice, and he can find these in the narcissistic leader. The narcissist's fearless-

ness gives her the ability to stand boldly against aggression, and her independence allows her to make decisions without the complications of relational attachment. She offers the strength and foundation her followers seek.

But leading out of your woundedness is a two-edged sword for your followers. I worked with a narcissistic leader who was impervious to criticism yet devoured any rival to her throne. She was brilliant at reading the fears of her staff and used that "empathy" to cement the loyalty of some while turning staff members against one another. Her favorite ploy was to "feel" the pain of her staff and then suggest how someone else in the organization was either the cause of the pain or insensitive to the struggle. She became the only source of comfort and solution. Seldom if ever was the staff person encouraged to deal with the problem or own his part in it. In short, the narcissist leader is usually brilliant in the art of gossip, the dynamics of office politics, and the strategy of divide and conquer.

Driven by emptiness and isolation, the narcissist creates cultures of idolatry. This self-absorbed leader craves having someone be fully and completely captured by his glory. No wonder leadership is appealing. It offers one of the best opportunities on earth to have power, control, and adulation, but only for a short season. Betrayal is assured.

Now it's a given that everyone is selfish and, at times, self-absorbed, but leaders surpass the normal levels due to earlier and deeper wounds they have suffered. As a result they struggle with being narcissistic. The greater the emptiness they have experienced, and the longer they fail to humbly name their demand to be idolized, the more power they will use to compel adulation from others. Narcissistic leaders tend to take more risks with bigger consequences than less-gifted colleagues. Followers who seek both the promise of safety and the allure of adventure flock to the narcissist's side—until the cost escalates and the benefits wane. Then narcissistic leaders are the perfect foil for the staff's combined disappointment and anger.

When the drama stops being fun, the followers scapegoat the leader who seduced them to follow his dream. They start a campaign of gossip and other passive-aggressive guerrilla tactics to take out the leader without much risk to themselves. That approach seems justified given how hurt they feel and how awful the leader now looks to them. In turn, the narcissistic leader grows more resolved not to care what the rabble wants. There is always another church or organization that needs what the narcissist offers—a ticket back to Eden.

The narcissistic leader I worked with was eventually let go by the ministry, but she is credentialed, articulate, charming, and masterful in job interviews. Within a month she found another job in her area of expertise. The board that let her go was afraid of a lawsuit, so no one in her new firm had an inkling of the emptiness and violence that walked through the door as its new CEO. At times it seems as though narcissists rule the world.

Self-Absorption: The Character Flaw of Narcissism

The term *narcissist* is often used to refer to someone who is a first-class pain in the rear—an egotistical, rude, self-absorbed person. But there are as many forms of narcissism as there are colors in the spectrum. We may be able to identify the most unattractive and malevolent forms of narcissism, but we are too often blind to its less obvious manifestations.

Narcissism spans a continuum. On one end is the malignantly cruel, disdainful, and powerful person. Farther along the continuum you pass the Type A, tyrannical, task-driven, win-at-any-cost, ambitious leader. At the other end you have the introverted, aesthetically elite perfectionist. Narcissism in any form involves the following four aspects:

1. Lack of interest in the perspective of others: *Why would I ask anyone a question unless I can use the opportunity to tell her what I know?* This is a failure of curiosity.
2. Highly opinionated: *Even those who agree with me don't understand what I see.* This is a failure of humility.
3. Emotionally detached: *To feel is harmful because it means being vulnerable and susceptible to the desires of others.* This is a failure of care.
4. Ruthlessly utilitarian: *Your value is exclusively tied to what you produce for me.* This is a failure of honor.

Despite these traits of narcissism, many people today commend it in its nonmalignant form as the basis of great leadership. Michael Maccoby, author of *The Productive Narcissist*, argues that a visionary leader (read: narcissist) evidences two core qualities: "A true narcissist is the kind of person who (1) doesn't listen to anyone else when he believes in doing something and (2) has a precise vision of how things should be."[1] Maccoby commends the visionary drive, the fearlessness, the charisma, and the endurance of the productive narcissists who are not controlled by either the prevailing paradigm or the whims of the masses. They are probably lousy husbands, wives, parents, and friends, but do you want fuzzy-wuzzy good feelings or success?

The problem is that success is not a matter of merely harnessing chaos and driving the troops to perform well. In the believing community, success requires shaping your character to the contours of the One who calls us to mimic him—Jesus. The antithesis of narcissism is Jesus, and any model of leadership that prizes even the secular notion of servant-leader must eschew narcissism in all its forms, virulent or benign.

True success involves failure, brokenness, and humility, but narcissists reject this notion. Humility is too similar to humiliation, which is a reminder of the betrayal they suffered in the past. Narcissists spend their lives avoiding further betrayal by refusing to need other people. But betrayal is inevitable, even in the lives of leaders who work hard at connecting with others, sharing power, and enhancing the capacity of their people. Someone will eventually turn against the leader. As the sad and cynical assertion reminds us, no good deed goes unpunished. Betrayal is certain; what is uncertain is how we will embrace betrayal and use it for the growth of character.

RELUCTANCE: THE TIPPING POINT TO REST

Consider the life of the prophet Jonah. God had used Jonah to bring his people to their senses, and he was a well-known and well-respected leader. But then God called him to do a vile thing—to go and preach repentance to the people he despised most. It would have been like Ralph Lauren being called to work as a greeter for Wal-Mart. It would make perfect sense, in that instance, for Ralph to flee to the Riviera.

Jonah fled to Tarshish to avoid the humiliation of being a prophet to the hated people of Nineveh. In midflight he was cast into the sea, swallowed by a fish, and unceremoniously spit out onto the shore. He reluctantly preached to the Ninevites and they repented. But instead of being humbled by all of this and rejoicing over it, Jonah turned dark and furious. The dialogue between Jonah and God is one of the most self-absorbed conversations in the Bible:

> But Jonah was greatly displeased and became angry. He prayed to the LORD, "O LORD, is this not what I said when I was still at home? That is why I was so quick to flee to Tarshish. I knew that you are a gracious and compassionate God, slow to anger and abounding in love, a God who relents from sending calamity. Now, O LORD, take away my life, for it is better for me to die than to live."[2]

The furious prophet-leader preferred death to being humbled. He refused to offer God's love to the renegade and the despised. His flight from God exposed his deep and abiding hatred of God's peculiar love for sinners, those who have betrayed and turned against him. We share Jonah's struggle. God calls us to live out his love, but we are an earthbound, sin-saturated people. So our furious flight from God reveals our petty, dark, self-absorbed cruelty. It can humble us. We may finally fully realize that we are not gifted, suave, powerful, and competent performers who demand respect and obedience. The fat folds of the naked emperor can now be seen by all his subjects: we are exposed.

In Jonah's case, as in ours, there was more to learn. One moment of exposure is never enough to transform us. Only repeat encounters with our furious flight brings us growth and, as I'll explain, rest. Jonah's story continues:

> Jonah went out and sat down at a place east of the city. There he made himself a shelter, sat in its shade and waited to see what would happen to the city. Then the LORD God provided a vine and made it grow up

over Jonah to give shade for his head to ease his discomfort, and Jonah was very happy about the vine. But at dawn the next day God provided a worm, which chewed the vine so that it withered. When the sun rose, God provided a scorching east wind, and the sun blazed on Jonah's head so that he grew faint. He wanted to die, and said, "It would be better for me to die than to live."

But God said to Jonah, "Do you have a right to be angry about the vine?"

"I do," he said. "I am angry enough to die."

But the LORD said, "You have been concerned about this vine, though you did not tend it or make it grow. It sprang up overnight and died overnight."[3]

Jonah created a place to rest, and God brought even greater relief from the heat through the shade of a sheltering vine. But after Jonah came to prize the vine, God killed it. Is this a punitive and capricious Zeus or the deadly serious, playful God who loves redemption more than life?

The narcissist believes that the world is rigged to harm, so she is committed to achieving a position of power in order to protect herself from more betrayal. But the God she serves sets her up, uses her, and betrays her by ruining her narcissistic dreams. God simply invites a narcissist to either rage or rest. Rage will leave the voice hoarse, the door frame cracked, and the hand bloody, but it won't change the peculiar heart of God.

The self-absorbed leader must face her fear and her folly in order to move from envy to reluctance. The benefit of running is that it magnifies our inability to escape ourselves. Run to the ends of the earth—the same internal war and the same battle with God remain. The only change is that now the warfare has taken on new geography. The narcissist will never find rest by imposing her will on others or by intimidating others through her rage. God, of course, cannot be ruled or intimidated.

We all rage against God, but narcissists stop there. When they have exhausted themselves in their fury, they crawl off to lick their wounds. They lash out at anyone who approaches, but they no longer bother with God. A limping leader is different: he will continue on, again and again bumping into the God who will not back away. Remember, only repeated encounters with our furious flight from God can bring us the genuine rest we seek.

God invites the one who rages to collapse in his arms of love. Rest comes when we can no longer sustain our flight, and we find God waiting for us. But rest is not true rest without surrender. For a narcissist, surrender is equivalent to being young and helpless; it is a return to the original wound of betrayal that gave birth to the fury to be in control. We must eventually be caught face to face with God and be unnerved by his kindness. Only then will we surrender.

The female narcissist I mentioned earlier in this chapter finally got caught. It was not by more job conflict, though that continued unabated. She got caught by the death of her father. He had not only sexually abused her, but he had put her on a pedestal and both worshiped and debased her. He used her wickedly and then rewarded her with glory. As a young child she was not able to see the dark potion of shame and power that he made her drink. She protected him and diminished any sense of the harm he had done to her.

Then he repented. On his deathbed and over the span of several weeks, he confessed his harm and tried to enter the harm he had done to his daughter. It nearly killed her. She later told me that his confession ruined her life far more than the earlier abuse because it exposed her shame and heartache and shattered the role she played as the highest god to be honored and the greatest whore to be violated. It tore down the illusion she had built around their relationship.

So she railed against God and against the worm that had eaten her illusion of comfort and control. Her father invited her to enter the agony of her emptiness and the presumption of her illusions. And God invited her not only to repent but also to open her arms to faith.

GRATITUDE: THE FRUIT OF HUMILITY

Leaders often possess large egos. Perhaps it takes someone with an abundant ego to think he can do what others view as impossible. Leaders typically blend strong vision with a deep dissatisfaction with the status quo. But they usually lead people who value the status quo and don't want to risk change. This setup for frustration can lead either to a rise in authoritarianism or burnout.

An oversized ego may also come from being fed the adoration of the crowds. No matter what the size of the pond, a leader is known and imbued with power. Furthermore, a high degree of entitlement can arise in the minds and expectations of leaders who seek recompense for the exhaustion and suffering of leadership. Men and women who make little money in their leadership positions often feel entitled to perks to help compensate for the long hours and constant criticism. That's one reason why leadership positions provide fertile soil for growing self-righteousness.

Self-righteousness is a trick by which we gain power, and the power comes with comparing ourselves favorably against others: *I may be overweight and less healthy than you are, but I am a harder worker and that is what really matters.* We naturally compare ourselves to others and come up wanting on many levels; self-righteousness seeks to give us a leg up on the competition. The self-righteous leader knows that she is successful because she works harder or is brighter or more gifted than her peers. She demands that others acknowledge her gifts, and she is critical of those who are less capable.

However, the leader who has fled, faced his cowardice, and then surrendered knows that his place is provisional and that his innate skills or gifts are insufficient for the task at hand. He serves as a privilege, not as a divine right. He is humbled because he knows that many others are more deserving of the position but that somehow, in God's irony, he has been allowed to serve as a leader.

I have a dear friend who works in a Christian college as vice president of development. Ever since he was a young man, he has longed to be the president of a university. He has served with great acclaim in a number of universities. He earned his doctorate and advanced to the position of vice president. His work was solid and good, yet his ambition pressed him to keep one eye continuously on the future.

This man is the antitype of a narcissist. He is kind and open. He builds consensus, blesses others, takes the blame for his failures, and bears the weight and responsibility for the fumbling of others. He couldn't be more unlike the narcissist described in this chapter. Yet he, too, struggles with self-absorption and a few narcissistic behaviors. We all bear certain narcissistic qualities, but the important question is this: to what extent do we face our self-absorption, our wounds, and our envy?

I had not seen my friend for nearly a year when we had a chance to dine together at a national development conference. I was taken aback by the transformation in his presence. He was more relaxed and happier than I had ever seen him. I asked what had transpired. He said,

I really have not had to work that hard to be where I am. As a result I don't think I've been very grateful. Finishing my dissertation nearly killed me. I understand now why more than 70 percent never finish that portion of the doctorate. I couldn't do it alone, and I refused to ask for help. The harder I tried, the deeper I sank in the mire. I hate to admit it, but I've been a proud man who is versed enough in humility not to let others see my arrogance. It was, of course, God's severe mercy. It took me several years more than was expected to finish the degree, and many asked when I was going to finish and I had to look them in the eye and say, "I don't know. It is far harder than I ever expected."

Each time I wanted to quit, my wife, who is wise and kind, helped me name my fears and call on a deeper courage than I thought I possessed. So I stumbled forward and I finished. The result was not a sense of pride but of deep gratitude. My perseverance was a gift. My intelligence is a gift. Even my breath each moment is a gift. I can't tell you how it came about, but I started to love my work more than ever. It isn't the next rung on the ladder. It is the place I am meant to stay unless God wants something else for my life. I know I would be a good president, but I don't need to be. I only need what he has given me, and that is to be a good man who does a good job in a work that is infinitely important. I am happy.

In other words, it is only by and through grace that we are meant to lead. And the grace of the moment is the manna for today. There are enough problems today *and* sufficient grace to meet them now. There is not grace for tomorrow because the gift is now, for the moment, and not for what is to come. There will be grace for tomorrow, but it will not come today.

Reaching this place of rest in leadership involves gratitude. In fact, when you live and lead with a deep sense of God's grace, you can't avoid gratitude. It's humbling to give God all the credit, and it's also a place of deep rest. My friend learned the power of gratitude and was blessed by it.

A narcissistically oriented leader begins his transformation to limping leader when he tastes God's invitation to mourn his past and present betrayals, to release the mistaken idea that this is the only place he will find comfort and rest. Also, the limping leader does not steel himself against connection and care; he risks involvement with others, because he has learned the value of kindness. And a heart that has received even a dollop of kindness knows gratitude.

The funny thing about gratitude is that it is not earned or deserved; it, too, is a gift. We can't force ourselves to be grateful, but we can stumble into the arms of gratitude when we're exhausted from our running.

Gratitude opens the heart to acknowledge one's gifts not with pride but with amazement and awe. It is inexplicably wondrous that someone with a heart like mine could be called to lead by offering another person the bread of life. Gratitude receives even betrayal as a gift that deepens our hunger for the manna of kindness.

ESCAPING SOLITARY CONFINEMENT

The Truth That Sets a Lonely Leader Free

Most leaders know what it's like to walk into a room and notice the atmosphere suddenly change. A leader is not an ordinary person because others view her through a lens of heightened expectations and desires. No matter how hard a leader wishes to be a regular person, it is just not possible.

Years ago as a young therapist, I went to the grocery store early in the morning to get milk. I turned down one aisle just as another shopper was coming the other way and we nearly ran into each other. It was a client with whom I had met perhaps three times. Her eyes bulged, her mouth fell open, and her face reflected sheer terror. To my horror she dropped two bottles of bleach on the floor, shrieked, and ran out of the store.

Seconds later an assistant store manager ran up and shouted, "What did you do to her?" The words came out of my mouth slowly and quietly: "I am her therapist." The manager took in my appearance—cut-off army shorts, a T-shirt, and flip-flops—and said, "Oh," and walked away. I don't know which reaction affected me more: his or hers. I realized early in my career that a therapist is not expected to shop early in the morning looking like a slob and that bizarre behavior is assumed if you earn your living as a therapist. I was not a normal person.

It is no different being the president of a company, a pastor of a church, or a leader of a women's Bible study. The moment we take on the mantle of leadership, other people assign us a power that can do them harm or good. Most leaders don't ask for such power over others; the power is simply given. And all of a leader's efforts to be normal only heighten the reactions of others. The pastor who has a beer with the boys is perceived as trying too hard to fit in. But if he turns down the offer of a beer, he'll be thought of as too good to rub elbows with the rabble. No matter what a leader does, it almost always will fail to have the desired effect.

In some research I conducted as I wrote this book, a number of "professional Christians" reported the feeling of being seen as leaders who wouldn't or couldn't relate to "real people." One pastor wrote of his deep loneliness:

> I love to fish, but only once have I been invited to go fishing. A number of men in the church fish, but they never ask. The same goes for golfing. I've asked others, but I never get asked. I think the problem is that I am put on a pedestal. I joke sometimes that my first name is *pastor.* My position causes people to fear me, and thus it is safer to keep me at a distance rather than allow me to get too close.

For this pastor, being set apart as a leader led to exclusion and loneliness. On the other hand, a leader's honesty about his struggles may bring an awe or respect that distances him from the very people he wants to serve. I once shared with a small group of pastors a terrible moment of conflict between my wife and me. Afterward, a pastor publicly thanked me for my honesty and vulnerability and added, "I'm sure what you shared is for the sake of illustration rather than what really happened. I can't believe you really failed your wife that badly." I was startled. I had purposely softened the details of the story, choosing not to use the actual language that had erupted between my wife and me for fear the pastors would write us both off as imposters of the faith. But even my toned-down account was too raw and too honest, so much so that this pastor found it threatening. He preferred to continue to think of me as "a leader" and not the chief among sinners. No one wants to believe that leaders are in such desperate need of the Cross.

Even the effort to deconstruct what people expect of a leader often just creates new facades that must be dismantled if truth is to be served. But the result for many leaders is a deep sense of isolation and loneliness that comes with realizing that others will never understand them or richly enjoy them. Many leaders believe loneliness simply needs to be endured as a cost of leadership, and others actually prefer to be alone, though they live with a low-fever loneliness.

Finally, most people think leaders are extroverts. How else can they get up in front of a crowd and speak with such winsome passion and power? But the truth is that many leaders are introverts who prefer to be left alone with their ideas. We have a professional class of pastors, usually megachurch level, who are brilliant speakers and tacticians, but many of them are uncomfortable interacting with a small number of people and prefer to delegate such relationships to others.

All leaders are lonely, but few are lonely for good reasons. The phrase "It is lonely at the top" is true, but it doesn't distinguish legitimate loneliness from self-inflicted isolation. There is a fine line between the two.

NO ONE CAN UNDERSTAND

A leader in a large parachurch organization told me a story that illustrates the bind of being the one at the top who has to make the hard decisions and thus endure aloneness. One of the most popular evangelists in this man's ministry had drawn many university students to the group through his passionate teaching and rich humor. That was all to the good, but the evangelist was deeply mistrustful of the organization's senior leadership. He undercut their authority when he spoke with staff and peer-level leaders. Repeated efforts to address the problem finally brought an ownership of his failure and a stated willingness to repair the breach. But then the same pattern repeated itself.

After confessing his sin, the evangelist would rebuild his base of support among students and others. Then he would find another reason to question the leadership. Two of his criticisms, for instance, were that the upper-level leaders were unwilling to take risks and that they were envious of his gifts and the spiritual fruit his life was producing. His critique was further cloaked in doctrinal differences. It was pointless to continue confronting the evangelist. He needed to be fired, but doing so would produce a major rupture. The senior leader knew the young leader might move to another ministry and take many of the students and perhaps even some of the paid staff with him. On the other hand, keeping him on staff would undermine the leadership and play havoc with morale in the organization.

The top leader also had been told by a confidant at the organization's national headquarters that the ministry at his campus might be phased out because of a lack of growth. This was not information he could share with anyone on his executive team. If he pulled the plug on the arrogant evangelist, the ministry would likely sink. But if he could wait until summer when the students were away from campus, he could let the young leader go without toppling the work. That meant coping with the crisis for another four months, but his staff was on the border of mutiny or despair, and he was gaining the reputation of being a weak and even naive leader.

Leaders often have more information than those they lead. And even if leaders told others of the crises and complexities of their world, they would receive only dull, blank stares. It is somewhat like bungee jumping. People will watch you jump into thin air, but ask one of them to join you in the feat and he will look at you like you have lost your mind...and he might be right.

Such is the case in dealing with the conundrums of leadership. People can't understand unless they have the cord attached to their ankles and are standing on the platform ready to leap into destiny. The ministry leader faced with the insurrectionist staff member shared his situation with two friends, neither of whom was involved in leadership. One said, "You just need to do the right thing and trust God for the results." The leader was so sickened by the counsel that he didn't bother to ask his friend what might be the "right thing."

The other friend was kinder but admitted he had never faced such a dilemma. He did offer to buy the leader a drink—a well-meaning gesture that indicated the friend's companionship would offer a pat on the shoulder but no meaningful counsel. The leader accepted the offer, and within twenty minutes his friend shared that his marriage was in trouble. A leader almost always is expected to be on duty. In this case, his friend's personal struggles outweighed his concern for the leader's plight.

No One Wants to Understand

We leaders all face the inevitable gulf that separates the world in which we live from the world inhabited by those in our organization. No one can fully understand us. What hurts more is that few really want to understand us because such understanding would call them to join the world—and the pain—of the leader.

Psycholinguists, those who study how we talk with each other, tell us that it is rare for a person to ask more than two meaningful questions of another person, especially if that other person is in distress. We want to help, to quickly resolve the struggle. But we don't want to suffer someone else's helplessness or confusion. If all we need to do is offer to move furniture or give a few dollars to settle the issue, then we willingly help. But to sit with Job in his agony is more than the vast majority of human beings will do, even for those they love most.

Sitting with Job in empathic silence is hard enough, but asking him to narrate the situation, listening with genuine interest and concern, and suffering with him as if the pain were our own—all of this is rare enough to be the Holy Grail of compassion. Such sitting with requires a bounty of time as well as skill born of one's own experience of isolation and a refusal to let another person suffer alone. Very few saints are willing to offer such care, and the result is that leaders simply stop wanting for it. After all, that kind of care just isn't available. So we stop letting ourselves feel lonely, and we toughen our skin and ignore the broken parts.

No One Is (Fully) Allowed to Understand

More than anyone else in the organization, a leader knows about matters that affect the lives of people he both cares for and relates to on a daily basis. He may, for example, know that a person will be fired as soon as a suitable replacement can be found. Whether he bears this knowledge alone or with a few select confidants, this information is a burden. It sets the leader apart from his community. At least 70 percent of the leaders I surveyed had experienced the isolation that comes from firing an employee and not being able to tell others why. Many said it was the most significant and complex work-related crisis they had faced. One woman who worked in a church said,

> Because I work in a peer-based ministry, I am often friends with people
> in my congregation. When someone is deeply struggling or we need
> him or her to step down, I often take a hit for not sharing details with
> my staff team or other leaders in the community. But I protect confi-
> dentiality, often at a personal cost to myself. Friends often feel that they
> should be in the know about others in the congregation, and I refuse.

Honoring confidentiality puts a leader in the direct path of the Mack truck of gossip. The tough decisions that can't be explained or defended leave leaders vulnerable and alone. On top of that, leaders often don't hear the scuttlebutt circulating among those they lead. A leader is often the last to know about things happening in the organization. Co-workers don't want to jeopardize their status or risk censure for telling the boss bad news. It is crazy-making to know more than most and less than everyone.

In this odd world of leadership, how is it possible for a leader to be a friend or to have friends? A leader with no close friends is a leader who is prone to swing between hiding and manipulating. That's why, if I could use only one factor to assess a candidate for employment, it would be the nature of the person's friendships—longevity, diversity, losses, and betrayals—and the candidate's desire to grow in the area of relationships. A leader will serve an institution no better than she lives as a friend. But one can't be a true friend without the capacity and willingness to allow the other to know something of her inner world.

The number one friendship, of course, is with one's spouse. It is the basis of the phenomenally strong statement by Paul, "If anyone does not know how to manage his own family, how can he take care of God's church?"[1] The word *manage* in the original Greek does not mean "to organize or administrate"; it means "to care." How can someone care for the church if she doesn't care for her own family? And why do most people pursue their families and spouses in the same way they engage in a diet—by fits and starts?

On the other hand, it is never righteous to be thoroughly absorbed with one's family. The father who is at every game and never misses a performance is not a good parent or friend; he is addicted. For many leaders, this kind of attendance record is not an issue; it is actually rare for leaders to be present even at a child's biggest games, let alone the practices. Refusing to stay at work, immersed in the adrenaline of crisis and the allure of being indispensable, takes discipline.

Leaders disagree about the wisdom of having friends in the organization. Working closely with good friends can create a conflict of interest. That's because a good friend is not merely a person with whom you spend time or share concerns and support. A friendship involves troth, or a pledge of fidelity. The word *troth* comes from the root word that is the same as the word *truth*.[2] Friends make an oath of loyalty to live in truth and to honor, protect, and provide for each other. Although this oath is rarely spoken, it is definitely assumed. We expect our friends to stand up for us, help us out, and not betray us. It seems inconceivable, then, to fire—or be fired by—a friend.

Add to that difficulty the fact that many staff people outside the friendship will feel envious of the depth of care and the long history of relationship between a leader and an employee who is also a friend. It seems much easier not to have friends in one's place of work, worship, or ministry. But we are caught in a bind. Ministry is seldom a nine-to-five job, so most of our human connections tend to be among those with whom we serve.

Having friends at work can be problematical, and not having friends at work can be problematical. People who avoid friendships at work usually do so because of the uncertainty, fear, and awkwardness of relational intimacy. This leads to a culture that divides the heart from the task, one's personhood from the work. The bifurcation of head and heart inevitably creates a culture of hiding and manipulative politicizing.

HIDING: THE CHARACTER FLAW OF MANIPULATION

We leaders hide when we are afraid. Someone at church asks us in passing, "How are you?" We understand the social convention, but at times we just can't say, "Great." We hint at the cold winds blowing inside, and the result is often polite distance. "Well, I'm sorry to hear you are not doing well. I'll pray for you." How many people do you know who would say, "I am so sad to hear you are not well. I have no time to talk now and I'm not sure you'd want to talk later, but I will call you this afternoon to check in." Since the latter group numbers so few, we leaders have learned to guard against hurt, even with friends.

Our commitment to hide too easily becomes our point of view, our barricaded castle. We experience the world through the lens of safety-wrought loneliness, and the result is a bind: the only way someone can get to us is by surmounting the castle walls, but the only person who scales a high wall is an intruder and probably a thief. This conundrum is similar to Groucho Marx's when he said he wouldn't want to be a part of a club that would have him as a member. A leader's potential friends are condemned in advance if they don't climb the wall—and they will be condemned later if they do. So most people don't bother to expend the energy when they know in advance that there is such a small prospect of success and acceptance. The bind that simultaneously beckons and repulses creates a crazy world. It is a treacherous minefield, and the only way to survive is to learn the manipulative trade of treading lightly.

Examples of How Leaders Hide

My greatest moments of loneliness come when I need someone who understands the weight and responsibility of leading a community. There is no one else in my church who has that experience. And as the only staff member, I don't have anyone in easy reach to talk with. Also, when large decisions loom and I want to talk with people and come to a group decision, most of our folks consider me the professional and say, "We're behind whatever you decide."

Most of the time no one knows how lonely I can find myself. My silence comes from not wanting to be perceived as whiney (even if it is my self-perception and not that of others) and not wanting to be seen as weak or needy. I can be vulnerable with other areas of my life, but this one I keep to myself.

I think I have become very good at disguising my insecurity. My guess is, if you asked most of the people in my community, they would say that I am strong and sure of myself. It's an image I learned to project a long time ago. I do it now by default—and probably also to avoid dealing with the issues that would arise with me and others if the truth were brought to light.

This account underscores a sad reality: no one can truly understand the weight that leaders carry on a daily basis unless he or she is in a similar position. It is too easy for people in a congregation to fail their leaders by assuming that the "professional" will take care of things—why else did we hire him? And it is even easier for a leader to hide his loneliness in order to keep others from questioning or disrespecting his calling. The result is not only greater loneliness but also deeper exhaustion due to the labor of keeping up the front.

Organizations are full of binds like this because there is not sufficient honesty between human beings to build caring, committed relationships. Instead, everyone figures out how to put on the right face. If it is a happy organization, then the faces people choose to wear will be happy. If it is an intellectual and serious place, then a happy disposition will be seen as superficial and naive.

We often learn what our culture requires and then set our disposition to the frequency of that world. Such posturing is a form of manipulation. It is a two-faced presence that both defends against exposure and fights for a position of power to keep from being vulnerable. The politicizing of power creates alliances and adversaries that collude and wrangle over issues as diverse as budget, organizational priorities, and office space.

In a particular season at Mars Hill Graduate School, I became aware that a small contingency of colleagues was working to silence my concerns about a particular decision. This realization had come on the heels of a lot of conflict and exhaustion, and my default mode at that time was to ignore the problem and keep my nose to the grindstone to finish writing a book. When the flood of tensions rose above my busy nose and I could no longer get any air, I began to address the politicizing of the decision and the sense that much had been said behind my back. My concerns were dismissed, and when I couldn't find any common ground with the people involved, I pushed harder. My energy was called paranoia, and with that label any more engagement on my part would simply prove their point.

This situation reminded me that the role of leader is inherently lonely because it often requires you to address problems when many in your organization would prefer that you stay away. When I put off addressing the growing tension at Mars Hill, I found myself in a lonely bind. I had been accused of paranoia. Did I want to be thought of as the disengaged leader or the paranoid leader? Neither option appealed to me. If I tried again to ignore the problem, it would gradually get worse. If I forcefully addressed the problem, it would quickly get worse.

It is times like this when the relational gulf between competing or conflicting individuals in your organization can be neither escaped nor resolved. It is one of the loneliest aspects of being involved in ministry, where one of the central tasks of godly leadership is to undermine all attempts to create false kingdoms that prevent people from serving the kingdom of God. One pastor named this task in these brilliant terms:

People in organizations form alliances. Loneliness in leadership that has integrity mostly relates to the need to eschew these alliances when they would conflict with one's integrity and values. Another time when loneliness is highlighted is when things follow an unplanned course into adversity and folks want to save their own hides. A true leader cannot just melt into the ground. She or he needs to stand and quite possibly intercept arrows—and that in vital areas!

So is it possible to have friends in an organization when your troth is to care more for the kingdom of God than their personal comfort or happiness? The answer is usually no because, unfortunately, friendships in an organization tend to be less about seeking truth together and more about building alliances that secure power and safety.

Furthermore, deceit grows in an organization when people feel like they have to hide in order to survive. The result of hiding is a labyrinthine litany of half truths and lies that eventually make the community cynical and mean. The mission of the organization is lost in the fury of people's fighting to keep power and avoid being exposed.

A dear friend told me of a moment in a staff meeting with nearly sixty employees when he questioned whether the company's penchant for high drama, intense work loads, and long, unpaid overtime was due to the nature of the business or more a by-product of a CEO who was brilliant, chaotic, and undisciplined. He said, "I might as well have asked whether folks wanted to be killed by lethal injection or hanging." Every organization has its zoo of unacknowledged elephants, and the unspoken rule is to not name what will make everyone uncomfortable. What results is a culture of hiding, game playing, and manipulation.

But a limping leader will act and speak in ways that violate unspoken rules. A leader can't hide if he is to undermine alliances that violate the integrity of the gospel. Yet how does he expose the truth about an organization that will upset many of its members and still retain their respect? It is a conundrum—but one that must be engaged. It can only be done by a leader who will openly confess his hunger for truth.

HONEST HUNGER: THE TIPPING POINT TO OPENNESS

Honesty is as simple as telling the truth. But telling the truth to another person is never merely a matter of stating that something is valid and beyond question. If my wife asked me, "Why are you so angry today?" and I replied, "I'm not angry. I don't know why you've been on my case the last few days," who is telling the truth? Is she more accurate or am I? Isn't each of us likely to be both right *and* wrong?

The issue of truth in relationships is never a matter of trying to figure out who is right and who is wrong. It is an issue of whether troth grows as both people seek the truth together. Truth is measured not only by how accurate the words are but also by how the words bind the hearts of those who seek the truth together. The more we seek truth together, arm in arm and heart to heart, the more we will gain a greater understanding of what is true. When we ask, seek, and knock, the promise of God is that our deepest hunger will be satisfied.

So if my wife accuses me of being angry and I defend myself or deny what she is saying, I have not only broken troth, but I am at the same time running from the truth. I don't have to agree with a person's perception to keep troth, but the more bonded we are, the more likely it is that we will see things in concordance with each other. Honesty is not just saying what we feel or think; it is seeking to be laid bare before the eyes of truth to see as we are seen.

What is true, honest hunger? It is the deep, naked confession that we need each other. It is perhaps the simplest acknowledgment but one that many husbands and wives, though married for decades, are unable to offer each other. To do so would be too dangerous. If your need for another is not received well or if it is betrayed, the pain can be excruciating. Rare as it is in marriage, the confession that we need each other is almost nonexistent in the formal structure of leadership.

The love of truth creates a deep hunger and humility to eat and drink more truth. And biblical truth is ultimately always about relationship, therefore, the more we partake of truth, the more we are drawn to hunger for the kind of relationships that are marked by a passionate love of God.

Imagine saying this to someone who is your friend: "I miss you when we're apart. I'm so delighted when we're together." Now imagine saying to someone who has hurt you: "I don't know what happened to divide us, but I long to be restored, and I would like to hear how you understand this struggle." If the first statement makes you uncomfortable, imagine going through with the second.

Honest hunger after truth requires us to remain open to everyone, including those with whom we disagree and have conflict. It also requires that we remain open to the fact that we desperately need the very people who challenge and contradict our cherished notions of the truth. We may never agree, nor do we need to do so, but we need others—especially those who challenge us to dig deeper and become more human. The hunger, then, is not so much for agreement on factual accounts, but more for troth that leads to a greater delight in the truth.

Troth involves an incarnational presence of care, honor, and delight in other people that values and serves them in spite of our differences. Where troth is real, a common ground exists for exploring both the facts and our interpretation of what we perceive to be true. Where troth exists, our interpretational differences will not prevent us from caring for one another, but our conflicting convictions may become more deeply differentiated and lead us to say it is best not to remain in the same organization. Or we may realize that the greater good is served by both of us remaining in the same organization because our tensions better model the potential of unity in Jesus than easy agreement on specific issues would.

But where exactly is the line between too much healthy tension and too little, and how can it be determined? It won't be found in a dark cave of manipulation, hiding, and incrimination. It can only be found in the context of needing one another—with all our weaknesses, our differences, and our irritations.

Becoming more human involves confessing one's need for others. To confess that I need you—to help me think through a decision or to have compassion on my struggles—is to admit that I am not enough, period. I am not enough, and neither are you enough for what I need, but together we are more than I can ever be alone. And to tell the troth is to remain simultaneously open and loyal to what the process will reveal.

Honesty confesses as well that the call to remain open and loyal is beyond my human capacity, especially in the midst of hurt or conflict. An honest heart acknowledges the insatiable human desire to be in union with others. It confesses that all connection with another is the only true home we can have in this world. Honesty in a relationship of troth causes the heart to tremble. And it is rare, tragically rare, that we enter into relationships of honesty with others where our desire for connection and our vulnerability in telling the other person of that desire causes us to tremble. Instead, honesty has been misused as a synonym for saying difficult things with little care for the other.

So-called honesty can easily degenerate into name calling, blaming, and judgmental critique. Too many people have chosen to say terrible things to others under the banner of "telling the truth." This is not honesty but cruelty and thinly veiled vengeance. Honesty promises to remain tender and kind, full of hope and desire for the other person's growth. The more we remain honest with the other, the greater our desire will be to know and to be known, to know truth and to be pursued and seized by what is true, by the One who is true. Honesty frees us to care.

CARE: THE FRUIT OF AN HONEST COMMUNITY

Honesty with troth fosters a community of care. The more honest I am with you about my alien life, the more possible it is for you to suffer with me and delight in me. I am an alien because I am not at home. At this point I am also an alien to the world that is to come. So I am at home nowhere—an alien to both heaven and earth.

But that's okay because it is not possible to feel pain for someone who is not an alien and a stranger. People can't reach out to a leader who is arrogant, self-sufficient, and independent; they can only reach out to people in need. Being cared for means that leaders must reveal their own suffering, so that others can enter the war that is in their hearts.

What then does it mean to be a friend when you're also a leader, and how can you avoid the self-imposed prison of loneliness? First remember that we invite and enter friendship to the degree we are willing to bear another's burdens.[3] We can't bear a burden unless we are aware of the other person's need. We can weep with others only when we know there are tears on their faces, and we can laugh only to the degree we are invited into the hilarity of their story.[4] The more honest we are about our alien lives, the more tears will be wept by others as a prayer for our redemption.

But tears alone are never enough to lower the volume of loneliness. We crave delight as well. A caring friend offers both tears and laughter. If all one is offered is sorrow, then it will breed self-pity and indulgence. We must also invite and offer the delight that comes as we celebrate another's life.

Care gives and receives both sorrow and delight. If you have someone who will weep with you, delight in the goodness of your glory, and confront you honestly and tenderly about your failures, then you are singularly blessed. No longer are you alone in the isolating work of leadership. Loneliness is no different from the growling of the stomach that indicates we need to eat. Loneliness invites us to return to those who weep and laugh with us. Loneliness is never meant to be the "cross" that leaders are to suffer simply because they are leaders. A leadership team is meant to be a community of friends who suffer and delight in one another. And to the degree there is a refusal to be friends, there will be hiding, game playing, politicizing power, and manipulating the process to achieve invulnerability.

Life is meant to be so very different.[5]

Worn to a Nub

The Exhaustion and Disillusionment
That Introduce True Hope

The week I spent at the Emergent Conference, a meeting of people who are asking how to live out the gospel in a postmodern world, almost undid me. After the six-day, seven-in-the-morning-to-one-in-the-morning gathering of passionate, gifted, and bright teachers and conferees, I was so exhausted that I left behind two pairs of pants in the hotel-room closet and a shirt in the drawer. I'm amazed I made it to the airport with my bags in hand and the clothes on my back.

I would have preferred a day or two of rest after the conference, but I was returning immediately to a week of twelve-hour days teaching counselors and lay leaders how to help people who have been abused. With my students, I had to step into the heartache and drama of abuse. In addition, the deadline for delivering this manuscript to the publisher was looming. I knew that whenever I had breaks during the week of teaching, I would need to write, and that in and of itself is a demanding and soul-wearying labor. Further, I had more than a hundred unanswered e-mails in my in box, some that were three months old. And then there were the organizational and personnel issues that awaited me after my week away.

Some people might consider all this a boast, but I write it as a confession.

The leader who doesn't feel pressed to the wall often is not involved in a work that is advancing sufficiently against the forces of darkness. But the burned-out leader has allowed the intensity and exhaustion of his calling to take away the pleasure of hope. Every leader is desperately in need of hope, but two factors entangle us: unlimited need and expanding opportunity. And those factors do their best to extinguish hope.

UNLIMITED NEED AND EXPANDING OPPORTUNITY

I was about to leave to go fishing with my son when an acquaintance called and begged for an appointment that afternoon. The area she wanted to address was in the sphere of my expertise, and her desperation was warranted given a conversation that needed to occur later that night with her husband. Immediately I was caught between two different needs, two different opportunities. A leader is moved by the interplay of these two dynamics. I must act; to do otherwise would feel traitorous both to the person who is in need and to my desire to do good.

The tug between this woman's desperate need and the less obvious hunger of my son to spend time with me left me feeling drawn and quartered. I chose my son, but I felt as if I were abandoning a drowning woman. The remainder of the day I suffered survivor's guilt as well as doubts about my own heart. It didn't help to remind myself that I am but one person and that the needs of the world are far greater than my capacity to meet them. It didn't help to tell myself that my son needs me or that I am not the only person on the earth God can use in that woman's life. I ached while I fished, laughed, and played with my son.

I got to thinking about all this. I realized that the felt need for action is commensurate to the intensity of the cry for help. The more need there is, the more action is necessary to respond to the opportunity. Yet the more we act, the less energy we have in reserve. The more energy we expend, the less we have to give. And until our reserves are replenished, we can't motor forward because our fuel has been depleted. It is a simple formula.

The challenge lies in the fact that need is energizing. A cycle of arousal begins with the awareness that someone is in need. We see injustice and are aroused to empathy and anger, and we prepare to enter the fray. God imbues us with adrenaline, noradrenaline, and catecholamine that fuel our energy so we can enter the stress zone. Read the words of some leaders:

> I actually thrive on the crisis moments because I've become very good at doing the interventions.

> Stress motivates me to work harder and longer, and it often inspires my creativity.

> I thrive under pressure and am at my best when things seem to go haywire. I am best at managing controlled chaos.

Leaders are drawn to the fight, but once we engage, our bodies suffer stress and exhaustion—and we can find that we're in over our heads. All the best-laid plans of mice and men can't ensure what will transpire. In fact, the only certainty is uncertainty and chaos. With any and every step forward, we find new demands on our time. I agree to speak at an event—a simple hourlong talk on a topic I have addressed before. However, the sponsor wants to see an outline. Then there's the phone call to go over the talk with the host, and he tells me that I'm walking into an emotionally charged environment: several staff members were recently fired, and others have resigned. The remnant is resistant to any outsider coming in. A simple yes to a speaking engagement leads to complexity I could not have imagined.

Every choice to do what you know you were meant to do—and to forsake the good things for the great things—will inevitably lead to new needs that present themselves as necessities. To reduce chaos and complexity in our lives, we must build in margins and set boundaries; we have to limit what we do. But the fact is that need is a wide maw, always open and waiting to devour us. And for too many of us, the only solution to exhaustion is to get busier:

I have to work harder during intense pressure because I can't think as clearly and don't have as much energy. So it takes more work and conscious energy. I tend to withdraw relationally until the stress has passed, which isn't necessarily good, since there are so many stressful times.

BUSYNESS: THE CHARACTER FLAW OF FATALISM

Being busy seems like the polar opposite of laziness, but a busy person is not so much active as lost. A lazy person does little to nothing while a busy person does almost everything, but the similarity is that both refuse to be intentional. Busyness is the moral equivalent of laziness.

The schedule that has back-to-back meetings seldom provides an opportunity to reflect, learn, and plan. Instead, it follows the tactic of "ready, fire, aim." I've attended far too many meetings where decisions are made on the spot with no time spent beforehand to ponder the agenda, read the information, or hear different sides of the issue. Why do we do meetings this way? Because we are too busy to do otherwise.

We say that haste makes waste, but the way we function indicates that we really believe that the hare, not the tortoise, wins the race. Exhaustion is inevitable when we take on too much or fail to anticipate the unseen demands that come with every new commitment. And our exhaustion plays itself out in countless ways, especially in our key relationships. Many of the leaders who responded to my survey lamented the effects of exhaustion on their families and their health. They may thrive on pressure, but they see it play out as relational frustration, fear, and despair:

When I am faced with intense emotional times in ministry relationships, I must force myself to be open to my family and friends. I become more tired and withdrawn, almost fearful that people will want something from me that I cannot give to them.

My response to pressure is to do all I can to meet the demands, but when the pressure is unrelenting, I tend to become hopeless and discouraged.

We are prone to a vicious cycle of first allowing our reserves to be nearly depleted, then further draining ourselves by using what little reserves remain in order to push through weariness to complete the task. This cycle of exhaustion feels inevitable, and often there really is no way out of the morass. When we reach that point, our exhaustion becomes a form of fatalism.

Fatalism is hopeless determinism. To the degree we surrender to leadership's inevitable demands, we become numb to the labor and turn ourselves into beasts of burden. The image of fatalism is the ox that plods endlessly around the same circle. I once worked on an assembly line where I tightened a screw on a part to ensure that it would not allow water to penetrate. The parts came at the rate of eight per minute. The pay was good, but within a few hours I stopped thinking or feeling and became another cog in the machine.

A fatalistic spirit merely endures the endless monotony of life. This may be the reason the average U.S. citizen watches four-point-two hours of television a day. Fatalism is also a central factor in our compulsion to overeat and drink. At least we feel alive when we're sated. Finally, rather than face how little meaning we enjoy, we succumb to the distraction of doing more.

Busyness, however, is moral laziness because it involves refusing to live with courage and intentionality. Instead we give our spirit over to the growing demands of necessity. What would happen if we said no? What would transpire in our workplace if we were to say, "Let me ponder for a day whether I can take on this task given what I think I uniquely bring to this organization"? What would occur if we regarded the inevitable needs facing us as opportunities for the discipline of intentionality rather than merely as more activity?

I suspect this approach would cost many people their jobs. After all, it would slow down the wanton progress of many institutions that fuel busyness so that no one has the time or presence of mind to ask the difficult questions.

In our culture and day, the benefits of greater reflection, wisdom, and excellence that increase well-being and longevity don't seem as valuable as frenetic movement does. Our use of noise illustrates this truth: we hate the quiet, so we turn on the radio or CD player as soon as we get in the car. We surround ourselves with noise and busyness so we don't have to look at the monotonous trap we have created for ourselves. We do so to avoid facing disillusionment.

DISILLUSIONMENT: THE TIPPING POINT TO HOPE

A busy leader spins webs of activity to satisfy an inner yearning for meaning and the hungry expectations of others. Our busyness has little to do with God. But its one benefit is that it eventually comes back to mock us and awaken us to our foolishness. Our frenetic pace will, in the fullness of time, reveal our threadbare souls. The revelation is not merely that we are exhausted and need a break. It isn't even that we are overextended and need more balanced lives. As true as those things may be, the truest revelation is that we have lost sight of our callings and, far more, of the One who calls.

The tipping point that returns us to our First Love is disillusionment about all our lesser loves. What originally led us to serve others by leading them seldom remains our North Star. The sole reason to serve as a Christian is Jesus, yet he is easily lost in the various activities that consume our days. The real cost of busyness, therefore, is the loss of our spiritual vitality. Among the leaders I surveyed, it was a common sentiment that crisis and pressure can energize activity, but they deplete the soul. It costs much in both time and desire to stay connected to spiritual resources—to Jesus—during those times:

> When the high point of the campaign was over, I realized I had not fed my soul well and was running on empty. The adrenaline rush of leadership in this area left my soul dry.
>
> I like the adrenaline rush of an intense period if it has a clear endpoint. I can usually prioritize the most important of the urgent items

and put off the less important. What tend to get short shrift, however, are the nonurgent but important items, including my own spiritual growth.

We may begin the day with Jesus and pray often throughout our demanding hours, yet he is elusive in the midst of a meeting. It is incredibly hard to make him the center of our discussion when we are making decisions, for example, about whether we should renovate our building or find an entirely new site. And as the intensity of the current crisis, decision-making process, or discussion rises, it is not obvious how to make Jesus the central factor in the moment.

One can be in a room full of leaders, all of whom love the Lord and desire to serve and please him, and still there can be terrible conflict between radically different views of how to resolve the problem at hand. Serving Jesus doesn't mean there will be unanimity of mind or heart regarding the resolution of a problem or the direction of an organization.

If Jesus is so easily lost in a group of those who love him, it ought to be obvious that he can also be easily obscured in the debris of our personal busyness and weariness. How does he reclaim his place as our First Love, especially when we so easily crowd him out in our efforts to serve him and others?

We move toward an answer to this question when we acknowledge that disillusionment comes when the thrill of the challenge wears thin. Most leaders love the adrenaline rush of intensity, and many leaders privately confess to loving certain kinds of crises and high-demand situations because they bring the same physical arousal as extreme sports do. Crises can become an addiction, and when a period of relative peace and calm comes, the absence of intensity can lead to boredom and irritation.

That's why some leaders unwittingly create new crises and drama at the first hint of peace—which, in their minds, is evidence of complacency and compliance with the things of this world. But adrenaline junkies, like any other addict, will hit a wall when the benefit of the addiction does not outweigh its depleting effect on the body and soul. When the body can no longer bear the weight, God begins to woo the leader's heart to a new way. We seldom return to the Father unless or until our supplies run out.

When we come to our senses and finally prefer the smallest role and the least opulent quarters, it is because we have lost our illusions. The illusion that drives most leaders is discontent-driven idealism. Seldom do leaders take on their burdens merely to maintain the status quo. A true visionary pursues a dream that she can transform what exists and create a better way.

Such discontent is exhilarating and identity forming. After all, each generation views the creations of others as incomplete and compromised: *If the leader who served before me had just had more courage, honesty, sincerity, passion, foresight, wisdom, or strength, then we would not be in the mess we're in now.* It is far easier to build a sense of who we are on the grounds of what we oppose than on what we dream of creating. Discontent-driven idealism does attempt to create a better world. Doing so, however, requires dismantling and rebuilding the old airplane engine while in flight. Organizational change is also a lot like starting a diet at a wedding. Everyone else is feasting and partying, and the temptation to return to the trough is profound. A leader is not only dieting but also trying to convince the other guests at the party to reconsider their food intake. If he is lucky, he will encounter no greater harm than being ignored, but he is much more likely to be tossed out into the street.

Therefore, the idealistic leader must wrestle change forward. He must not only diet but also teach, preach, and write about a better diet. He must lose weight, be healthy, and love tofu. He must both bear ridicule, gossip, and patronizing treatment and ignore innuendo and personal affront, all the while attending dinners where everyone else devours greasy ribs and sodden french fries.

Such a leader, energized by a measure of arrogant discontent and narcissistic vision, can't help but eventually run headlong into the thick, heavily fortified wall of reality. Followers want change only when they aren't happy and usually when it doesn't require much risk or sacrifice on their part. A leader seldom marshals troops who are willing to sweat, let alone die. One can speak of vision and mission, calling and opportunity until the cows come home, but when the day ends, most people want nothing more demanding than some television and a few uncomplicated laughs.

The illusion of discontented idealism convinces leaders that people, when they are given a good cause and quickened motivation, will rally to the cause. This illusion causes leaders to believe that change is possible if we can show our people but a glimpse of the Promised Land. This lie is seen as so Christian that it can't be allowed to die. We believe the lie is our only hope for growing Christian organizations. But the lie must die if we are to lead with a limp.

Remember Moses? Before he led a nation, he wandered in Midian for forty years and tended sheep. Our days spent in the desert may be shorter, but they will be no less agonizing because they are a season of death. A leader's dreams must die if a deep soul is to be born. Idealism may get us into the fray, but it is the loss of all we cherish that begins to form in us a heart capable of leading others reluctantly and humbly.

Disillusionment is not the end of dreaming. It is merely the end of our current reason for getting out of bed and fixing coffee. Disillusionment takes us to the question: what does it profit a man if he gains this world and loses himself? And disillusionment exposes that while we were supposedly serving the kingdom, we somehow became the king, and when we thought we were following Jesus, we inexplicably made him a servant of our dreams. The only real tragedy is the leader who never allows disillusionment to wear him to a nub and expose the godlessness of his busyness.

A pastor wrote the following about his exhausting schedule. More helpful even than some practical counsel he received was the pointed realization that no matter how hard he works, he is not God.

When I served as the vicar/pastor of a mission congregation with an incredible set of developmental needs while also attempting to complete a degree in ministry, I was overloaded to a point that I have never been before or since. While I seemed to thrive after a fashion under the stress, some wiser and more seasoned mentor ministers injected a powerful dose of sense into my mind by warning me of the consequences of unremitting intensity. Included in their list was increased short-temperedness with those who did not deserve such treatment. I now know in retrospect that I am not God, not even a god, and that I certainly cannot perform as all the pressure points would have me perform. I do not have to respond to everyone's agenda, not even my own. I have learned—or rather am still learning—the limits of authentic leadership.

Despair begins to resurrect a hope that is not based on striving performance or the rush of success. After all, hope found in any human creation is a form of planned obsolescence. Our national economy is built on the necessity of purchasing either a newer version of what we bought last year or a replacement because fixing the old one costs more than buying the new. We could not sustain our country's financial growth if products lasted. We expect things not to last.

We are not that different when it comes to hope. We hope that the best-selling book or the new movie that depicts the gospel will be the silver bullet that wins our culture for Christ. The blockbuster *Passion of the Christ* was touted as the biggest hope for evangelism since the rise of Billy Graham. A year later the film was barely on anyone's radar screen. So we are starved for drama and quantitative proof that something is happening for God's kingdom. We hope in the newest program, the newest manifestation of the Spirit, the newest new thing.

But becoming disillusioned over everything that is new and better—and all that is planned, programmed, produced, and promoted—allows a new hope to grow, a hope based on the coming of Jesus and the promise of a new heaven and earth. This hope allows us to be far slower, more deliberate, less grandiose, and more intentional about what we will do and also what we will refuse to sacrifice in the name of achieving a vision. Disillusionment will make us both bolder and more paradoxical leaders.

Boldness: The Fruit of Paradox

Disillusionment births true hope in the same way that death is the context for resurrection. If our dreams don't die, then God-dreams won't be birthed. We know this fact to be true, and we despise it. The fruit of disillusionment-birthed hope is a loss of earnestness, a tapering of ambition, and a huge dollop of playfulness. It is usually described as "taking oneself far less seriously," and it has nothing to do with indolence or apathy. In fact, the disillusioned leader cares more and gives more—and does so with greater boldness. This growth all arises from the paradox of death-resurrection or dying to self to find oneself.

Clearly the disillusioned and best leaders are those who have nothing left to prove because they have known both failure and success. Failure teaches us to not fear the contempt of others. Success teaches us to not trust the applause of others. When contempt and applause no longer move your heart to hide or to strive, then you are ready to ask the question "What will please you, God?"

My understanding of what that might be is open to constant revision and transformation, yet it allows for a boldness of vision and a singularity of focus. I can't teach a class, prepare two sermons a week, visit several folks in the hospital, put out fires on the elder board, respond to eighty e-mails a day, raise funds for the building program, finish writing a book, do the urgent work that was left undone by a depressed colleague, return twenty voice-mail messages, and coach my son's baseball team. It is not possible to do all of this and still live out what God has called me to do.

Obviously, many churches and organizations can't afford to employ a truly bold and paradoxical leader. Such a leader is not bound to the pulse of busyness and, therefore, will, by how he lives, confront and expose the silliness of those who pay his salary. Why would a harried and exhausted congregation, for instance, pay to see its pastor live a focused and paradoxical life? The fact that he has time to read, pray, and weep is more than a driven and overworked parishioner can bear. Off with his head!

If we are bold leaders, then we compel people to reconsider the cultural norm that says, "Get it while you can! Push yourself to the limit!" The assumption for many is that you must make hay while the day is long and rest when the evening comes. The problem is that the evening has its own exhausting work. Therefore, there is really no rest except retirement. If you work hard and invest wisely, perhaps retirement can come when you are in your forties or early fifties. This philosophy is similar to hoping to avoid bankruptcy by winning the lottery. It is a fool's existence, one submerged in fatalism.

The inverted reality of limping leadership, however, is that disillusionment does not breed fatalism, but hope. Idealism pushes leaders into every battle in an effort to right all wrongs. Over time this idealism pushes a leader to the wall, exposing and clarifying her limitations. The pain of hitting the wall comes with seeing one's idealism suffer a mortal injury. The hope that results from hitting the wall comes with the realization that disillusionment frees a leader from the demand to do more today than was done yesterday. The hope that renews and refreshes limping leaders comes with the freedom of knowing one's limitations. When you admit that you can't do everything, you are then free to more fully embrace the call of God.

The beauty of a limp is that it slows you down, it forces you to take more time, it prevents you from doing as much as you'd like to do. The paradox of death leading to life requires that you disappoint many to please One. It requires you to say no much more than you say yes. It invites quiet at a far deeper level to help you discern what noise you can most wisely and profitably enter.

God calls leaders to combat evil and to do good. Hope focuses their work in conforming to God's call.[1]

10

Defining Your Calling

Three Decisions You Make as Chief Sinner

Every leader has to ask: *With all that is before me, will I continue to lead? If I choose to continue, how will I lead in a way that engages the hearts of those I serve?* If we are to engage the hearts of others, we must step into a profound war: every heart at one step wants to serve God, and with the next step prefers to escape into a life that is much safer and far saner. And if I continue as a leader, what defines me, really?

What words best describe a leader? The list you create will shape both what you do and who you become. The list can be endless: *hero, sage, seer, hearer, mouthpiece, fund-raiser, coach, catalyst, optimist, truth teller, surgeon, consultant, midwife, shepherd, visionary, CEO, general, parent, friend.* Each of those nouns was mentioned by at least one leader when they were asked, "What is the single best word to describe you as a leader?"

Likely each descriptor is accurate and good, but not one leader offered the words I hope you will consider: *broken, foolish, reluctant, hungry, or disillusioned.* The words given in response to my survey are nouns—solid and understandable. The words I'm asking you to consider are adjectives—fluid and foreign. A leader might be a fund-raiser or a field general, but what *type* of leader is she? Is she foolish, broken, reluctant? Nouns describe objective roles, parts to play, scripts to follow. Adjectives are more amorphous and qualitative, describing how we put our unique mark on an expected role. Both nouns and adjectives are necessary.

So consider not only what is expected of you as a leader but also *how* you are to lead. You must decide whether being the chief of sinners, a title Paul claimed for himself, is part of your calling of biblical leadership. Second, if you agree that chief-sinner status is essential to biblical leadership, you must choose to adopt that identity for yourself. Finally, you must enter the process of deciding when and how to live out being a leader who limps. These three decisions will define your calling.

THE FIRST QUESTION: IS IT TRUE FOR ME?

The Grand Inquisitor in *The Brothers Karamazov* by Dostoevsky rages against Jesus for not taking away human freedom. His argument is that Jesus honors humanity with choice and increases human suffering as a result. If Jesus had only taken the power to rule the world offered to him by Satan during the wilderness temptation, then we would be at peace and not caught in the heartache of life.

> The Grand Inquisitor says, "Had you accepted that third counsel of the
> mighty spirit, you would have furnished all that man seeks on earth,
> that is: someone to bow down to, someone to take over his conscience,
> and a means for uniting everyone at last into a common, concordant,
> and incontestable anthill—for the need for universal union is the third
> and last torment of men."[1]

The temptation for all leaders is to encroach on human freedom and take away the suffering of humanity through some form of authoritarian order. Indulging this temptation underlies the fascism of all utopias. Removing human freedom is done with sincerity and the desire to serve the forsaken and bent brood of humanity. But all of this is a lie. If limiting human freedom tempted Jesus before he began his calling as the Christ, then it will conceivably be an ongoing temptation for all who fall into leadership.

Fyodor Dostoevsky offers a more eloquent version of *The Matrix's* choice between the red or blue pill. The red pill will throw you into reality with all its pain, but the blue one will enable the illusion to remain intact and you to be happy and comatose. Which pill will you choose—red or blue?

The good news is that a leader doesn't have to make a choice between being a coach, shepherd, or midwife *and* being broken, foolish, reluctant, hungry, or disillusioned. Instead, our choice is whether to add to the more acceptable nouns of leadership the adjectives that point out our limp. Will we allow troubling and humbling words to enter our lexicon of leadership? Will you be a disillusioned midwife, a foolish shepherd, or a broken coach?

In the Bible God's leaders were a troubled and exasperating lot. The disciples were still waiting for an immediate political reversal of fortune even after Jesus ascended into heaven. Peter didn't understand the offer of grace to the Gentiles until long after Jesus departed, and he still needed to be confronted by Paul regarding his collusion with the party of the circumcision. And, as we have read, Paul referred to himself as the chief of sinners.

Is it true? Is living out the gospel in this world meant to be marked by an inverted, paradoxical, mysterious twist on what most people expect of a leader? Yes! God calls leaders to be servants. And we are to lead our organizations from good to great by serving, by giving credit to others when success occurs and by accepting the blame when failure ensues. I support the work of Robert K. Greenleaf and Tom Peters on servant leadership, but isn't there something more about the nature of Christian leaders? Is it possible that being a servant who is humble is just the beginning of the race? And is the next step, then, living into a paradox that is as disconcerting as inviting leaders to put on clown's makeup before entering into the day's labor? Is it true? You must decide.

THE SECOND QUESTION: IS IT ME?

Whether you fell into leadership in accordance with the model most often employed by God or you carefully planned your rise to the position, this question remains: *What do I most desire?*

A dear friend who leads a ministry of counseling and mediation recently wrote me and asked, "What keeps you going? What encourages you? Why would you remain in the madness when you can make a living somewhere else?" She has modeled maturity and a passion for the gospel for many years. When I asked her why she was asking such questions, she said, "I'm ready to quit almost every day. I just wondered how you remain faithful for another day."

Every leader worth his salt is asking the same questions. The task is ridiculous. The obstacles grow daily. Past employees spread lies and gossip or threaten to sue. Current employees are reluctant to take necessary risks. Leading others is a house of mirrors and a madhouse, a three-ring circus combined with an animal farm and a firefight.

But when I imagine winning the lottery and think about what I'd do with my windfall, I always return to the reality that I love what I do. I may wish to do less, but I don't want to do something else. And I can't pretend that I am anything other than Mars Hill Graduate School's chief sinner. I know some of the other sinners in our shop, and their candles burn brighter and clearer than my flickering light does. But I also know that God doesn't break a broken reed or snuff out smoldering flax. I am a mess, but I am more grateful than I am discouraged, more in awe than confused, so I can carry on another day.

Every leader has to face whether he will carry on with the status quo and merely retain the form of the organization or whether the radical inversion of the gospel is not just true, but true for him. For most leaders intellectual assent is not enough; change must be birthed in the crisis of conscience and calling. One must *choose* how he will lead.

THE THIRD QUESTION: IS IT NOW?

We are all procrastinators. Many things need to be done today that I won't get to legitimately, and by my procrastination, I will choose to delay other things. The way I manage my days is similar to the way I choose books for my nightstand. If a book makes its way to the stand, it has achieved a priority that few accomplish. I select my books with the discrimination of a Broadway director.

I don't care what sacrifice was required to get the book published; I care only whether the book is worthy of being on my nightstand. Even then I will read only forty to sixty pages to determine whether I will invest the hours to finish it. I may not make great choices, but I am discriminating. Yet each book I read requires saying no to some other worthy read. It is all a question of what ought to take my heart right now.

You may agree that walking with a limp is not only true but that it's true for you as a leader, yet you then decide that now is not the time to implement any changes. To start limping now may cost you a job that is crucial for gaining experience necessary for landing a better position in order to better tell the truth. Of course you could also be lying to yourself. Our motivation—even when we do what is most true—is mixed at best. We may tell the truth because we are angry about the years of lost passion and purpose. But not telling the whole truth may be a wiser course with a community that barely can admit that life is not one blessing after another.

There are definitely times when a little now and more later is the wisest and most honorable course of action. At other moments, though, gradual change will not be tolerated because a crisis has come that requires immediate and dramatic transformation. A limping leader must choose wisely when to come out of the closet. Vet the decision with your spouse and dear friends; seek their prayers and blessing.

I counseled a woman who was a partner in a prestigious law firm. She told me how the tensions among the partners were wreaking havoc in the organization. Everyone was burned out, yet they were still taking on more difficult cases than the infrastructure could handle. Her marriage was teetering on the border of disaster, and she knew that a number of other employees were barely making it through the day.

She shared her burden with a group of women with whom she prayed. She read the Scriptures and novels. She laughed and wept. She discussed with her husband the cost of speaking up at the next stakeholders meeting. They knew it could be the end of her well-paying job.

She had worked so hard to achieve her position that at first she refused to be the one to blow the whistle on the firm's idiocy and arrogance. But my work with her in counseling helped her see that telling the truth is never weak but that it actually requires courage and audacious faith. She finally told her partners that she didn't understand who or what was driving the reckless mismanagement of personnel and resources. She also asked if the out-of-control ambition of the firm was due more to greed or to arrogance.

The firm's older partners stared at her as if she had turned traitor. She told them that she had no intention of resigning *or* continuing to work the inhumane hours. She also wondered out loud if anyone else wanted to see their marriages and children suffer due to someone else's greed or arrogance. She told about her dreams for her children and husband, and she acknowledged the lack of courage she exhibited when she continually told her family that she didn't have time to be mother or wife. Clearly this woman chose not to lie or hide. She limped out of the meeting feeling like a fool, but she knew that her soul was more important than gaining the whole world.

This woman's courage was the catalyst for a month-long reconsideration of what cases the firm would take and how to redistribute the work load and financial remuneration. She still works with the same firm and is one of its most highly respected attorneys not only for her courtroom performance but also because she told the truth to her peers.

Is now the time for you to become a limping leader? Perhaps making that decision requires more reflection and prayer. Or you may wait until you are cornered before you decide to cross the Jabbok to meet God. In one sense it doesn't matter. The time will come, and you may let it pass without choosing to limp. Rest assured that another opportunity, like an approaching cloud on the horizon, will follow that one. Your opportunities to limp in this life are endless, and it pleases God to orchestrate those for his glory.

The remainder of this book assumes you have decided to embrace the paradoxical, inverted life of a limping leader. So what does it really mean that you are your organization's chief sinner?

11

THE PURPOSE
OF LIMPING LEADERSHIP

Forming Character, Not Running
an Organization

A leader who limps subverts the expectations of those who define leadership as running an organization. It is not that a limping leader does not hire, fire, advance, reward, discipline, and delegate. These are inescapable duties of leadership. But the aim of a leader's activity is not the growth of the organization. It's not even meeting needs or doing good. The purpose of limping leadership is the maturing of character.

As you may be well aware, the bigger-versus-better argument was fought in small and large organizations for most of the twentieth century, and it spilled into the twenty-first. It is a binary argument, and as such it misses the obvious point that numbers often grow when something is offered that touches the heart. In the words of the argument, bigger happens when better is provided. Consequently, many churches attempt to provide that which is better: day care, youth programs, Christian scouting, small groups, seeker-oriented preaching, convenient parking, and gymnasiums with small bowling alleys.

Even in the church, "better" has become a consumer-driven concept. We ascertain the hot issues and the most winsome ways to win over the largest number of customers, clients, or congregants. In doing what is better, however, a more important value has been given the backseat. Perhaps in the work of growing the organization bigger through doing better, leaders lose sight of the goal of growing character.

Leadership is all about character. I am a character. I have character. And as a leader, I'm meant to be part of the transformation of your character. The word *character* comes from the Greek word for "stylus." It is an instrument used either to carve a piece of wood or to mark a piece of papyrus. It carves, marks, and shapes.

All leaders must have character and must embrace their character. I have a role to play in the story of God, which means I *am* a character. At the same time, I am to play that role with integrity and grace, which means I *have* character that can be measured as good or lacking goodness. My character is good to the degree that it grows Christ in other people.

GROWING CHARACTER

The purpose of all life is to present every person mature in Christ. Each human being is meant to become like Jesus—and to mark other lives with a beauty that draws them to Jesus. The scope of that calling is so enormous as to be beyond comprehension. It means subsuming every dimension of life from how I eat and drink to how I vote under that one goal.

No wonder we attempt to separate the sacred from the secular. It is far easier to call certain behaviors civic or secular and then allow other activities to be uniquely religious. But the Bible won't allow it. Everything we do has the potential of giving glory or shame to God.[1] It's no wonder that we work so hard to figure out the "Christian" way to do life. For one large section of the Christian community, that means voting Republican and opposing homosexuality, women in church leadership, and Bill and Hillary Clinton. Others believe that the Christian way to do life involves spiritual disciplines, such as prayer, contemplation, fasting, and giving. Still others focus on supporting agendas or organizations that do a Christian good, such as feeding the poor, building strong marriages, coming alongside the broken, or evangelizing.

I counseled a man of immense wealth who is the champion of several national Christian ministries. His marriage was crumbling, and he sought my help. When anyone asks this man what directs his life, he readily answers, "Knowing Christ and making him known." His life goal is to have all things submitted to Jesus, though he acknowledges that he fails daily in achieving this goal.

During one counseling session I addressed this man's tyrannical and belittling behavior toward his wife. She was present in the room, and as she listened, he sprayed me with a barrage of self-justification. When I pressed against it, I was told that I simply didn't understand the extent of his wife's failure. He argued that I had been swayed earlier in the counseling session by his wife's stated willingness to change. Around and around we went until I called his self-righteousness ugly. Then he stormed out of my office, flinging invective and leaving his wife with no way to get home.

This lion of industry and faith is a thoroughgoing narcissist whose wealth and power have shielded him from hearing anything that goes against the grain of his empty, indulged, and fragile self. He has been in fellowship and Bible studies with many famous Christian leaders, none of whom has ever called him on how he treats his wife and his subordinates. Neither have any of these leaders asked him to tell the stories from his childhood that oriented him to being empty and brutal. No one has attempted to grow his character outside of the conventional structures of right voting, Bible study, and organizational loyalty. And I believe this is the case for most Christians.

What exactly does it mean to grow character? Character is grown to the degree that we love God and others. Love that is true and eternal begins with worship of the God who redeems people by his unexpected and unreasonable grace. We grow in character, then, to the degree we are captured by gratitude and awe.

Gratitude

All of life is a gift, and we grow to be like Jesus as we embrace this gift. I need only lift my eyes from my keyboard to see my wife. She brought me a cup of coffee as I was working on this chapter. And that's not all. We're on the Big Island of Hawaii, and I'm sitting on a lounge chair overlooking the azure Pacific Ocean. The view is breathtaking. And I know that every breath, each heartbeat is a gift. Not a single molecule of what I see is deserved or earned. The matchless gifts of my wife, of beauty, of the sun, land, water, and air that surround me make any presumption of ownership or entitlement completely laughable. All is a gift. And if the material, tangible world is a gift, how much more so is the embrace of our resurrected God?

Now, growth in character occurs to the degree that we accept being forgiven as a greater gift than life itself. If the greatest gift is not what I see but how I am seen by the living God, then my gratitude knows no limits. It can grow immeasurably as I suffer through the loss of illusions, the death of dreams, and the shattering of success. Suffering grafts our heart to grace.

In light of this gift of forgiveness and life, what am I to be? The answer is as complex and as simple as the gospel: I am to be free. The fruit of gratitude is freedom from death and its countless cousins—fear, shame, estrangement, and more. And what grows from freedom? A playful, curious connectedness to the unveiling of new grace in pleasure and in sorrow. To those who have eyes of gratitude, all senses are freed to take in and participate in the smallest and most obscure as well as the most panoramic displays of beauty. Gratitude also frees the heart to suffer fury against that which mars beauty. Gratitude brings an imminent passion to all endeavors of life.

Consider this sharply contrasting picture: I recall being at a birthday party for a five-year-old terror who snatched his gifts from his mother and opened them with wanton disdain. He'd see what he had received, toss it down as if it were of no account, then move on to another present. His mother wanly tried to stop his juggernaut by saying, "Isn't that wonderful, honey? Why don't you say thank you to Uncle Joe and Aunt Susan?" The boy had no gratitude, in part because nothing brought him surprise or awe. His sense of being owed the good things in life prevented him from being delighted by the undeserved gifts he was receiving.

It is impossible to be truly grateful without having some degree of awe. Just now my wife not only brought me coffee, but she also put her hand on my shoulder and spoke kind words. It was a simple but unexpected gift, and I was amazed. If we *expect* a gift—such as a birthday present—then we may be pleasantly surprised, but we seldom experience awe.

Awe

Awe is the capacity to bow in the presence of something or someone more glorious than ourselves. It is the proper posture of a creature before both the Creator and the Creator's greatness as expressed through creation. It is the experience of rushing to get a glimpse of a staggeringly beautiful sunset and remarking to a total stranger, "Isn't that breathtaking?" We prostrate ourselves before greatness because we were built to admire and honor glory. Awe is similar to envy but without envy's desire to possess or mar what we can't have or be.

I will listen and marvel for hours to the music of Ashley Cleveland or Lamont Hiebert. I may have heard a song fifty times, but the nuance of one syllable will finally capture me, and I feel awe that I can be in the artist's poetic presence even if only through the mysterious etchings on a CD. The mystery of presence is meant to take our breath away and remind us that each breath is not of our making or something we can control.

Each syllable of awe is meant to prepare us for the day we will stand face to face with utter glory—the very presence of God. To ride in the front of a roller coaster or to sit four rows from a virtuoso violinist performing a miracle on strings is a form of purgatory: it purges us of mediocrity and arouses us to desire something beyond ourselves.

Whereas gratitude calls us to be fully ourselves by embracing freedom, awe invites us to be fully part of something bigger and more glorious than ourselves. It is the mystery of other-centered sensuality. We feel pleasure not solely for ourselves but also for the sake of the other. We feel delight in giving to the other. There is no loss of self as we give to someone else, and there is no absorption of the other person. Instead, there is a regard for the other that gives us great joy as we bring all we are to serve that person.

What does it mean, then, to grow the character of the other as well as our own? It involves being committed to all in life that leads to gratitude and awe rather than to the things that birth presumption and control. What you think you deserve will turn you into a slave; what you think you can control will devour you. Growing maturity demands that we expose false gods and invite our hearts to desire what only God can offer.

If your heart is full of gratitude and awe, what impact will this have on whom you vote for or how you use your money? The presence of awe will allow you to regard your vote or your use of money as an honor, as a privilege to be used with humility and openness, not with pride and dogmatism. You, therefore, approach every context as an opportunity for conversation with those who know more than you do. Awe enables all of us to confess daily our desperate need for a greater wisdom and glory than what we have today. We will one day apprehend God face to face; today we are given a gracious glimpse of his back. Each encounter with glory stirs a deeper desire for more. Therefore, we are called to be lifelong learners.

Leaders are called to lead with character. And leaders grow the character of others to the degree they bless the character God has written them to become. We can't grow glory in another person without embracing our own.

BEING A CHARACTER

"He is such a character," she said with exasperation. It would have been so different if my lunch companion had said the same sentence with whimsy or delight, but her words were accusatory. I knew that, from her standpoint, his character was not an asset.

The expression "She is such a character" is spoken positively about only a few when God means it to be used that way for every person on earth. We all are given roles, characters, to live out on the stage of life. God calls us to live out our characters in order to reveal something about the character of God. Character reveals character. Character sets the stage for the unique role we are to play in revealing the story of God.

When I was researching and writing this book, my dear friend and colleague Stan Grenz died unexpectedly. I ate lunch with him two weeks before he died and asked him about his experience of teaching at Mars Hill Graduate School. He said, "I love the fact that we dream big, very big dreams, without any fear of being seen as foolish. We will fail at many of the things we are trying to do, but only because we have risked to dream far beyond what most others have considered reasonable." I was deeply touched by his assessment, and I asked, "Why do you suppose others don't do so?" He leaned forward and said in a hushed and conspiratorial fashion, "Most other seminaries don't hire a fool to be the president."

You would need to have known Stan to feel the fabric of his words. He was an immensely respectful and kingly man. He was brilliant and witty, common and corny. He could quote Luther in German, translate it into English, turn it all into a silly pun, and then return with great care to the heartache being discussed. His remark about my being a fool was both a gift and a warning that I still have much to learn.

There is not another Stan Grenz on the face of the earth, and there will never be another like him. What a wealthy man I am to have known him. And it is no different with any person of character.

To be a character requires gratitude for one's uniquely carved being. Do we delight in the strengths that are fearfully crafted into our characters? Do we bless how those strengths wondrously serve others? If we are not aware of our fearful and wondrous potential, then we probably aren't troubled by our failures or grieved by how we harm others. When we see the glory we can achieve, our choice of dross over gold will break our hearts.

Our calling, however, is often shaped as much by our weaknesses as by our strengths. We tend to run with our strengths and avoid those people and tasks that expose our weaknesses. But the story of God is not a saga of human potential; it is the revelation of the kindness and passion of the Father who seeks and redeems sinners. Therefore, our strengths may help us with certain tasks and opportunities, but it is our frailty and sin that make known the glory of God's story.

The story of Sandy Burdick, the seventy-something director of SALTS (Survivors of Abuse Leadership Training Seminar), the most successful lay training program to address sexual abuse, illustrates how our weaknesses become God's strength. When Sandy was the director of women's ministries in a church, Sandy and her husband, Bill, sponsored a Wounded Heart Seminar in their church. Participants expressed that they had discovered their stories of abuse during the seminar. Sandy asked me what to do about it, and I suggested she have a small group. A group of woman joined her to review the material and began to tell their stories, then realized that there were many abuse victims who needed a safe place to walk through recovery.

Sandy was soon immersed in the subject, and more women heard about her willingness to talk about issues that most choose to hide. Her ministry grew until she was helping train leaders to run fifteen groups for women and five groups for men.

Sandy Burdick is a kind, thoughtful, easygoing leader. She hates conflict and is not a rabble-rouser. She would have been thoroughly happy to have remained a director of women's ministries in her church forever. However, she was forced into a fight, not merely for SALTS, but for a safe place for the wounded. Legalists in the church voiced concepts that re-abused hurting people: "Just read your Bible more and pray." "You need to forgive and forget." "Psychology is heretical." "A woman can't teach the Bible when a man is present." Many in the church believed victims needed to recover in twelve weeks or less.

Sandy Burdick is not only a reluctant leader, but she was also ill prepared to lead what she began. She has a high-school diploma and three years at the University of Michigan and is not interested in building an infrastructure to run a ministry. Many have come alongside her to build the organization that now trains men and women as widely divergent as Orthodox priests, indigenous American and Canadian peoples, and Bosnian refugees.

She is enthusiastic and perseverant. She didn't ask for the ministry to abused men and women, and it cost her dearly when she chose to leave her church in order to stay involved with those who had experienced the betrayal of abuse. Perhaps the hardest part of her work was facing her own abuse as well as the struggles in her marriage and with her children. It was as if a Pandora's box from hell were opened. She stepped into evil's line of fire.

Sandy did what a fool would do—she didn't quit. She let the conflict with her husband lead to more honesty, and they began marriage counseling when they were in their sixties. She didn't ignore the heartache with her children but encouraged them to step deeply into their struggles with their parents and one another. The result of this courage is sweet redemption for the whole family. Bill now leads small groups for abuse victims, and several of Sandy and Bill's children are also involved in leading small groups for abuse victims.

The glory of Sandy's paradoxical frailty and strength is that it has enabled many in her community to pursue both greater humility and greater boldness. She is a living conundrum: a wise fool, a courageous coward, a sinner saint. She is a living embodiment of "already and not yet."

Our sin, our failure of love, makes the story we live a gospel story rather than merely a successful and helpful story. We don't need to fail or sin on purpose to create a good story; we fail and sin quite naturally. This reality leads to a major leadership paradox.

A leader—whether in the home, church, business, community, or government—has authority due to her role, but her positional power will not bring about good for individuals or organizations unless it is backed up by the capital of character. You may obey a leader who has power and authority, but you will not strive to serve her or the cause of the organization unless you respect and care for her in addition to the ones with whom you serve.

A leader is called to go further than anyone else. As a therapist, I know I can take no one any further than where I've chosen to go. I can never ask or expect a client to be more honest, more humble, more forgiving, or more sacrificial than I am willing to live. Wherever I stop in the progress of growth is the unseen line dividing civilization from no man's land. Consequently, if a person desires to lead others into maturity rather than mere productivity, he must go first. Otherwise, the discord that comes will derail forward movement.

But again there is a conundrum: I must go first toward maturity, and I will inevitably fail. I desire to treat the customer as the greatest priority and to serve the other as Christ. But how long will it be before my first failure? Perhaps I will be consistent for an hour or a day or maybe even a week, but I will eventually invalidate whatever value I hold, because I am a sinner.

What is the standard secular response? "No one is perfect; just do your best." This is well-meaning but hollow encouragement. My best is not good enough—ever. If it were, we would have world peace, and we wouldn't have to wait in line to get a table at our favorite restaurant. Something more than my best is needed. That something is the truth about who I am. I must confess that I am prone to wander, fitful in my loyalty, more likely to backbite than to offer grace—and that I am self-serving rather than committed to your good.

What benefit comes with naming what is true like this? The more honestly I name what is true about myself, the less I need to hide and defend and posture and pretend. And the freer I am to accept help from any source, the greater will be my gratitude for any sacrament of kindness I receive and the more I will desire to give grace rather than to make others pay for their real or perceived failures.

So a successful leader names his failures—without being a confession junkie or inviting pity from others. Admitting failure opens the realm for discussion and a plan for movement that addresses the harm without minimizing the injury. Acknowledging our failures is an opportunity to clear the air and open a new path for resolution.

The more I mature, the more I understand the high and holy glory of Jesus and how far away I am from his beauty. When I was much younger, I thought I was considerably more mature. The older I become, the more I am utterly amazed that anyone as screwed up as I am is allowed to be in the ministry at all.

This is not hyperbole: I am Mars Hill Graduate School's chief sinner.

Admitting such a thing can backfire. It can fuel a flight from others or launch a headfirst dive into a vat of self-contempt. Yet opening the door of the heart to the power of forgiveness makes the potential misuse of confession worth the risk. After all, as a chief sinner I am called to reveal the patience and mercy of Jesus:

> Here is a trustworthy saying that deserves full acceptance: Christ Jesus came into the world to save sinners—of whom I am the worst. But for that very reason I was shown mercy so that in me, the worst of sinners, Christ Jesus might display his unlimited patience as an example for those who would believe on him and receive eternal life.[2]

HAVING A CHARACTER

A leader must understand her unique blend of strengths and weaknesses, a blend that reveals the character of God, and then she must tell her story often and well. A leader is first a storyteller. She tells the story of her foolishness, redemption, reconciliation, and restoration to God and others. She is the canvas that God paints to reveal the beauty of his grace.

The better a leader tells the stories of grace in his life, the more he invites others to consider their own stories and calling. The more wholeheartedly he chooses a life of gospel passion, the more effectively he will call others to goodness. In that sense, a leader either has a character of goodness or not. There are indeed characters whose effect on others is to discourage or derail. They don't live with integrity or authenticity. But a person who lives out his calling to reveal his character invites others to freedom, kindness, and strength.

The church spawns many good-hearted people who don't know their own character. Therefore, they invite others to a life that is little more than middle-class politeness and cultural decency, mildly seasoned with a plenitude of Bible verses to justify a comfortable, bourgeois existence. When asked, "How do you uniquely reveal God? How does your story shape how you reveal God?" the answers tend to be "I have the gift of administration," "I teach Sunday school," "I love teenagers," or "I give regularly to my church." We are not used to thinking about our character and our role except in terms of what we do. We seldom consider our role in terms of *how* we do what we do.

I am a seminary president. But I am also, according to Stan Grenz, a fool. What did he mean? Well, he knew that prior to coming to Jesus I spent many years as a salesman of illicit pharmaceuticals. In this capacity, I spent considerable time raising funds to purchase more inventory. I learned to be persuasive and persistent. I also learned how to use a .9mm pistol. But even more, I learned that most people are afraid to admit both who they are and what they want. They are afraid to even take the risk of going after sinful dreams, let alone visions that move the soul. My experience in the drug trade taught me to take huge risks with my life and safety because a conventional life didn't seem worth living. I am eternally grateful for what I learned as a wicked man; it continues to shape how I live as a graduate-school president.

My character is a superb fit for a start-up, edgy, academic world, but I'd be a trapezoidal peg in a round hole if I were to try to teach or administrate in a traditional academic world. Even more, I'd be a gaseous element in a world of solids if I were to try to pastor a traditional church. I am a character, but to live well and to do good, I must live out my character in the right situation. Otherwise the disconnection between my role and the needs of the immediate community would be so great that I would appear to have little integrity or any heart for good. Sadly, many people have attempted to play out their unique role in a theater production that was a mismatch for their character. They flopped not because they didn't live well but because their unique strengths and weaknesses were not apropos for the context.

A leader, therefore, needs to ask these questions: *Who am I? Where am I meant to serve? How am I to use my gifts and suffer my weaknesses for good?* A good story is one in which I co-create with those whom I serve. We are meant to be a community that loves the stories of our great need for the gospel, the stories of celebrating the glory of grace, and the stories of how we have come to be who we are. Indeed, our stories of risk are the tales that tell who we are longing to become.

12

THE COMMUNITY OF CHARACTER

No One Grows to Maturity Alone

Stories guide us in defining who we are, how we got here, where we are going, and what we must do to get there. Stories form the raw material for the development of our unique mission and vision or, better said, for the development of our unique culture. Every organization is a culture with its own language, ethos, and brand. The culture orients individuals to the organization's values and shows how they can be in accord with its purpose and perspective.

And where does the leader fit in this culture? Every leader is a storyteller who narrates on behalf of the community the core reasons for its existence.

To get a sense of the importance of cultural stories and their power to shape character, consider how elementary-school students are taught about our country's founding fathers. Every student is told about George Washington cutting down a cherry tree. When asked later if he had done so, he replied, "I cannot tell a lie." Usually this is followed up with a story about honest Abe. The moral of the stories: We are a nation that tells the truth. We don't harbor lies, so you'd better tell the truth just like our forefathers did.

To take this illustration a step further, we are a nation that is a light to the world. We not only tell the truth but we also live it. Consequently, we have an image to uphold and values to promote that define who we are. President

Reagan, the master storyteller, used the image of a city on a hill as a means to restore the luster of our glory after the cynical seventies that followed Vietnam and Watergate.

These stories, however, fail to acknowledge the dark and deceitful means by which we became a morally superior nation. We stole our swath of North America from its original inhabitants, and then we sequestered the indigenous people on land that is, to this day, mostly inhospitable. And we kidnapped massive numbers of Africans from their homeland to perform the backbreaking sweat-labor of planting, hoeing, and growing our nation's infrastructure. It is not a noble past no matter how many times we invite the Indians to our Thanksgiving Day feast or listen to Motown or rap music. It is a history of presumptive and self-righteous theft that puts might before right.

The United States is similar to the respectable-looking family down the street that harbors incest and alcoholism behind closed doors. The family's public face is hard working and morally upright so that the story told is not the story lived. The story line has been edited and rewritten to hide the sin that cries out to be named and forgiven.

Why is Thanksgiving a feast instead of the time we admit our theft of the land? Why is there no holiday that remembers the violence committed against African slaves? The reason is that greeting-card companies and supermarket chains could never sell enough cards, hams, and turkeys to warrant a holiday when the day to be remembered calls us to grieve and repent.

What is true of a nation and of families will shape the ethos of the culture, including the church and other Christian organizations. And since stories shape our identity and calling and, therefore, our character, we must work hard to tell stories that are not sugarcoated. We must tell the truth, the whole truth, and a whole lot of the ugly truth.

A community of good characters must tell honest and compelling stories in order to become a transformative community. Unfortunately, what most organizations offer instead of good stories is spin. Stories have the power to shape character; spin is a story without soul or suffering, a story which consequently creates hypocrisy. Spin is of the devil.

THE DECEIT OF SPIN

Spin attempts to tell a flawless story with sizzle and panache, whereas truth is always more complex and gray. Spin puts padding over the jagged edges. The place where spin most readily spins out of control is in the realm of relational crisis, such as someone's being fired.

Personnel law prohibits employers from telling the story of a person's employment record or the reasons for his or her departure. Unless the departure is amicable, it is shrouded in secrecy and silence, and the vacuum usually fills quickly with acrimonious gossip. For a season the wound bleeds away the organization's vitality. To staunch the hemorrhage, many leaders turn to spin.

We tell the congregation that Brother Jones will be pursuing other ministry opportunities, and we bless his endeavors and wish him the best. A tea will be held in the church library after the next service so parishioners can say good-bye. I have been there both as the one fired and as the one who has done the firing, and it stinks on both sides of the river. Little can be done in the moment either to tell the truth or to make the departure less painful, less gossip-ridden, or less destructive.

What *can* be told, however, is the truth about not being able to tell the truth. We could say, "Because personnel law forbids it, we cannot tell you why Brother Jones is leaving. But we can tell you that we all have labored to address this matter with honesty and kindness. None of us has handled the process without some hurt and misunderstanding, but there is agreement that brought us to this end. We ask that you not spend precious time speculating or passing on information that has not been sanctioned by the elders. Let us instead live into this moment with prayer and kindness."

A congregation or an organization must understand both the benefit of confidentiality and its possible misuse as a screen to hide an unconscionable misuse of power. Departures are inevitable and need to be acknowledged as a part of the recalibration of every organization. However, we should become wary if departures are excessive or if they are initiated by only one person or a very small group of people. No organization ought to be run by an individual or self-appointed committee who can dictatorially hire or fire with impunity.

Now I have a couple of questions for you: Have you ever heard a sermon about how to end as well as one can when the ending is just not good? Or when have you heard a pastor, talking about being fired from another church, touch on the very things that led to his removal and detail what he learned from the experience? In both cases we spin instead of speaking forth truth.

Spin is also an effort to advance an organization. Consider that any new development, such as building, hiring, or growing, requires a period of preparation to help people understand why new chaos and sacrifice will be necessary. So the bugle rallies the troops to hear stirring speeches, vague plans, and the drumbeat of war. This is spin designed to enlist support and open pocketbooks rather than to paint a realistic picture of the challenges, obstacles, opportunities, and uncertain domain of tomorrow. Leaders who rely on power and authority prefer certainty—and spin offers it—in order to get people on board with their vision.

Seldom do we hear of the high personal cost of change or the possibility of failure. There will be little or no mention of the major obstacles to be faced or the specific plan for addressing those impediments. Consider the spin offered to U.S. citizens on the taking of Baghdad and the liberation of the Iraqi people. We were told, "The Iraqis will be dancing in the streets. They will greet us as liberators." The high probability of a prolonged insurgency was never acknowledged. Disbanding the Iraqi military set back self-determination by years. It was a huge mistake but was never acknowledged by the military or the Bush administration. Why?

The answer is simple: no president can continue to wield influence over Congress and retain the confidence of the American people if he acknowledges a serious lapse of judgment. We live in a culture where the acknowledgment of wrong or the ownership of risk and failure is paramount to forfeiting the game. The only way we can survive is to wink at personal failure and publicly offer a different face. This is called hypocrisy.

In Greek theater an actor held a mask on a stick in front of his face to portray a particular emotion or character. The mask set the context for what was about to be said. Using the mask came to be called *hypocrisy*, or "having two faces." Later the word came to mean "duplicity." Spin is a form of hypocrisy that tells only what can be stomached by those who hear.

I'm convinced that spin is also a form of brainwashing. Think about the confident assertions of political commentators. We hear something in the news and think, *That's bad*, but then a commentator puts a spin on it and we see that it's really not so bad. Spin softens our righteous anger and dulls our resolve to take action. Because, of course, we don't *really* want to have to take action. Spin gives us the excuse to not act because it tells us that things probably aren't that bad.

We listen to a public servant or a minister of the gospel talk about a problem or a potential gain, and we know we are not hearing the story of the raw reality of the situation. We are hearing instead the smoothed-over rough edges, the "truth" made palatable. A limping leader, however, chooses truth over spin. A leader who limps must tell stories that offer what Francis Schaeffer used to call "true truth."

THE FREEING BURDEN OF TRUTH

Truth is sure and strong, and when it seizes us, we inevitably become vulnerable. The truth ought to surprise us and make us weak in the knees. That's why I can best encounter truth in the context of community. Otherwise I won't have someone to help me bear the freeing burden of truth.

Truth stands before us as the righteous and glorious light of God, yet it is ridiculously easy to suppress. It takes little more than a word or a euphemism to banish truth. For example, I caught my son practicing his guitar rather than preparing for his French final. I spoke to him with strong and uncompromising intensity. He said to me, "You're being so mean. I was just taking a ten-minute break." I walked away from the interaction knowing that I'd overreacted but denying that I'd been mean. It was easier for me to say to myself, *I'm just ticked off,* rather than name that I was furious with my son for squandering his opportunity to improve his grades.

If I had faced the truth that I was livid, then I would have been forced to do more than shrug off my irritation. If I had told the full story, then I would have been pushed to begin to name all the things that I feel I've lost in life due to my own failure to perform well in school. My fury at my son, which I denied by using the euphemism "ticked," allowed me to escape the heartache in my own story. I fled from truth with a simple word.

Truth stands before us. She is fragile and inviting, yet relentless and unwavering in her passion to free the heart. We will not risk entering into truth unless we are surrounded by a community that seizes the opportunity to name the truth and then to stand with the one whose knees buckle when faced with truth.

The author of the book of Hebrews wrote, "But encourage one another daily, as long as it is called Today, so that none of you may be hardened by sin's deceitfulness."[1] We are meant to encourage one another daily. If we don't do so, the concrete of sin will set and the patterns of self-protection will harden. Sin will then both define our personality and our way of handling the uncertainty and struggle of life. We are meant to be stirred daily to love and good deeds. Without that, the good food of our soul will settle to the bottom of the pot and burn.

The price for stirring the pot in people's lives, though, is often a backlash from those who don't want to be invited to repentance and faith. A commitment to living in God's glorious truth makes us a target for slander from those inside the organization who fear and hide from the truth. To admit we are foolish, weak, and in need of repentance gives the vindictive and self-righteous camp plenty of ammunition to turn against us and to turn others against our leadership. But the alternatives to living in and living out truth are far worse: we either hide from truth or we choose to spin our sin and our story.

Hearing Your Own Story

We can't offer our story to others unless we are aware of the bigger-picture context of our own story. Character is formed in the midst of hearing and telling the full story. And in order to better comprehend the story of God, a leader must first enter into his own story.

Since you were there when your story happened, entering it would seem like the easiest thing in the world to do, but actually nothing is more difficult. The reason is we only know—or let ourselves know—part of our story. We hold on either to what we wish to remember or to what serves us well to recall, and we flee from the parts of our story that most deeply expose and unnerve us.

In addition to hearing your own story, though, you also must step into the stories of others. A leader can't intrude into the private life of others by inviting them to tell their stories in a manner that is reserved for a counseling session or a discipleship group. But there is a value in a leader's knowing something of the stories of the people she works with. It is good to know a bit about what has shaped others, where they feel called to grow, and whether in the present they tend to deal well or unhelpfully with others.

But again, a leader must first walk into his own narrative. If he plunges into his own story, then he will understand better where he refuses to live with faith, hope, and love. He will better be able to name how he attempts to make truth serve his own idolatry rather than allowing the lies of his life to be exposed by the searing goodness of God. We lead others to God only to the degree that we are aware of how much we flee him, how little we truly desire him, and yet how God is also the deepest, truest, and sweetest desire of our hearts. In the midst of this tension, we can live in the truest truth.

Soon after the interaction with my son occurred, I told the story to a few staff members. I wanted their prayers, but I also wanted to invite further discussion of how easy it is for me—for all of us—to use words to escape the truth. It was a profitable discussion, and later in the day a person many would assume was many notches lower on the organizational chart came and asked two simple questions: "Why do you suppose it is so hard for you to bless your own story when you've achieved so much? What do you still need to accomplish that keeps you from being able to bless your own life?"

They were gracious questions. I knew it would take much time and reflection to engage them, and I told her so. Then she asked, "Do you want to know from those who work with you when you do the same thing to us that you did with Andrew?" I was honored by her pursuit and blessed by her courage. In the many years since that interaction, she has encouraged me at times when the weight has felt too heavy to bear. Stories shared and entered—even to a small degree—weave our hearts together for a greater good.

THE TENSION OF TRUTH

Growing character in community requires entering into the tension that we want the truth yet we don't want it. Pursuing truth with others regarding our growth in character requires us to be willing to be caught in this enormous tension.

Perhaps the greatest tension in ministry is that most people have not signed on to grow, let alone grow through encounters with their stories and the stories of others. If the truth be told, most Christians define growth as learning how to stop doing bad things or finding new ways to avoid bad things. If a person fails occasionally and does only a *few* bad things, then growth is not compromised. If a person does a few good things, like going to a small group or reading the Bible fairly regularly, then growth is a given. Few people take growth to mean that we are literally to become like Jesus, which is very different from wearing a WWJD bracelet and thinking about trying to do what he would do.

To be like Jesus means that we must enter the complexity of both dignity and depravity. We are made in the image of God—glorious. We have taken on Adam and Eve's hiding and blaming—ruin. We are glorious ruins, bent glory. And it shows up in every moment of our existence until we one day see Jesus as he is and become pure as he is pure.

A pastor I know well is in the middle of a building program. Before they began, he confessed to his board what everyone already knew to be true: space was at a premium and they needed to build, yet a strong motivator to build at that time was the fear that a number of big givers in the church might be leaving in a year or two. Further, the pastor acknowledged that he felt a great fear of failure whether they did or did not build. He also felt he was in a bind between the attendance numbers growing (a reason to build) and his sense of success (not a reason to build). He asked for prayer as he confessed the war in his soul.

The board was stunned. The pastor had named both the goodness of building and the factors in his heart that would mar the project. He didn't deny the rightness of moving forward, and he acknowledged his own obstacles to leading well. He confessed both his dignity and his depravity, and he did so without self-pity or sabotage. He spoke with a voice of strength and mercy for himself.

The result was astounding. One of the board members who was wealthy and planning to move to a different city admitted he was not in favor of the building because he didn't want to be asked to donate when he knew he would be moving. The pastor pursued truth by inviting that board member to reconsider why he would be reluctant to give since he had been a founding member of the church and would likely be returning to the community often even if he moved. Others began to voice their ambivalence and fear, but before the evening was over, the commitments to build together with prayer and to acknowledge the issues of their hearts became as important as the building itself.

To grow character, we must not deny or hide from the reality of our unique dignity. We are made in the image of God, and we are uniquely woven with awesome beauty. We may be remarkably handsome or bright, possess great musical ability or a hysterical sense of humor. We may possess remarkable abilities to encourage others or to read the nuances of relationships. Whatever marks us with glory, we are meant to prize it and use it for the sake of others.

To grow character, however, we must also not deny or hide from the reality of our depravity. Each of us has a unique way of hiding shame and blaming others for our failures. We must admit the truth that we are a mess and that we mar everything we do with some stain of the Fall. We are meant to grieve this and to repent. We are both awful and awesome at the same time. Leaders must be able to see, name, and honor both dignity and depravity in all their endeavors.

Leading people requires throwing yourself into a process that is fragile and tension-filled in order to help them not only do their jobs and fulfill the organization's mission but also grow as characters with character. We must serve them by telling stories that clarify why we are doing something and how we are to do it, and we must tell these stories with the goal of growing the character of the individuals and the organization.

PARTICIPATING IN TRUTH

All systems—whether a family, a megachurch, a for-profit business, or a group of friends that meets to talk and pray about starting a coffee bar—must engage in a process of character development through story. The process that best grows character and vision is one that moves from exploration through dialogue and discernment to decision making. Leadership is telling and listening to stories in order to birth new stories.

Exploration

Exploring is the honeymoon stage of leadership. Generally it is characterized as "getting to know you." Seldom are pressure and rigid expectations imposed. Whether it is the first six months of being on the job, starting a project with a newly formed committee, or having lunch with a new acquaintance, the exploration period is one of ambling discussion.

The work of exploration is an attempt to scan and appraise the terrain: *Who are you? Who are we? What will we do, and how will we do it? What needs to be done, and how can it best be accomplished?* It's like a first date where both parties are trying to gauge what the future might hold by seeing how well the present moment works out.

Here's what I mean: I met with a woman who may lead a significant dimension of our graduate school. Her skills and work history were impeccable, and her credentials had been thoroughly investigated and discussed by others on our committee. I was to tackle the question of how she might fit with our culture. On a warm Seattle morning, we sat down outdoors for a lengthy breakfast. The discussion moved from conventional questions about our backgrounds and histories to issues of the unique good and ill of Mars Hill Graduate School. I attempted to name both the dignity and depravity of the school and of the school's chief sinner: me. The goal was twofold—to offer her an accurate picture of the graduate school and also to ask how she has operated in similar contexts.

Exploring is simply asking the first existential question in the Bible: "Where are you, Adam?" Exploring asks: "Who are you? Where are you/we going? What do you/we want? How will we get to where we want to go?" The only requirement for exploration is that both participants engage in an honest exchange.

Yet the truth, the whole truth, and nothing but the truth will not be told by any party in an interview or conversation with someone who is not a long-established confidant. Does that fact mitigate the possibility of significant, honest discussion? I believe honesty is not the core goal in this situation. Instead, a leader is looking for this process to reveal, through honest exchanges about life, how the other person takes in data and uses it to engage the matters at hand. This exploration is best done when human dignity is loved and honored. If dignity is honored, the truth will eventually be told.

Dialogue

Dialogue carries exploration into the realm of interpretation. When we explore, we do so with a set of biases or presuppositions. We are aware of some of these, but we have never named most of them. There is no neutral discovery of data that eventually gets formed into a theory. Instead, we see everything through a lens that orients us to what is important and needs most to be seen. That's why we must submit our way of seeing to others who see the world through a different set of lenses. Doing this is uncomfortable and scary, but it's absolutely necessary if we want to better see the world.

Dialogue is different from discussion, and it also differs from debate. Discussion is merely the sharing of ideas on a topic. Debate is an attempt to sway or dismantle the ideas of another. Dialogue stands apart from both: it is far more opinionated than discussion and far less adversarial than debate. Dialogue requires you to approach the matter at hand with a viewpoint—a way of seeing reality—and the desire to have that viewpoint tested, refracted, and re-formed. It requires that we hold in an open hand cherished notions of ourselves or truth. Dick Averbeck, an Old Testament scholar, is fond of saying, "When I approach the Bible, I always begin with the question: What is wrong with my understanding of this text? What is wrong with me that this text wants to reveal?"[2] He acknowledges that he has a bias and invites Scripture and the Spirit of God to open his heart and eyes. He extends the same invitation to those who engage in study with him.

This approach honors depravity by acknowledging our need for the eyes of another: I can do nothing that well on my own; I can do almost everything better once it has been submitted to community dialogue. Dialogue, however, is not merely a matter of listening to someone else's opinion and factoring it into one's own. Dialogue involves a push and pull, a hammering and stretching that inevitably causes pain. Being challenged or questioned can prompt us to hide or assign blame. Being told that our idea or project has significant flaws exposes to us the underbelly of our narcissism, and we must have fortitude and commitment to remain in the process.

So what do we do when dialogue tests our assumptions, questions our methods, challenges our motivation, and invites us to go back to the drawing board? For me the process is similar to having my writing edited. It's exposing, painful, and humbling. And it's even more so when I read what I've written aloud and solicit face-to-face feedback.

The process can seldom be done well with people whom you don't respect or trust. If there is a breach of care or suspicion of ill will, the dialogue will not be collaborative or expansive; instead, it will be suspicious and judgmental. The process will result in one-sided attacks or assertions rather than an all-hands-on-board working together to take an idea to the next level of beauty.

Good dialogue tends to create more chaos and confusion than clarity. It tends to expand the realm of possibilities, both good and ill, that needs to be taken into account. It pushes the community to take ownership of ideas and plans because they are jointly created even if one author wrote the first draft. Now, with all the new potential and chaos teeming, dialogue must submit itself to discernment.

Discernment

One of the least utilized tools for developing individual and corporate character is discernment.[3] It is not that we don't discern and make decisions, but often we don't do so as a formal, intentional process. Instead, we let the exigencies of a meeting bring forth the data (exploration), we debate a few of the options, and then we either default to postponing a decision, we let the leader decide, or we make a group decision. What happened to discernment? It is usually lost in the wash of busyness.

Often a group will pray and ask for the Spirit's aid in the process, and individuals may ask God for help. But these prayers still are not sufficiently communal. They require little of those in the group but to bow their heads and nod assent. The process of discernment requires time and trust. Questions must be pondered: Which option most honors the unique character (calling and story) of this person or organization? Given the current situation, what will allow this person or organization to best live out that unique calling and mission? (This process is necessary, but tragically it can become a form of coercion or manipulation. It is crucial for people not to pronounce the will of God for another person or to impose their will as a divine prerogative.)

Discernment is another word for dreaming on behalf of others. It calls us to ponder what this person or situation would be like if God were the center of desire, the sole purpose for what we are deciding to do. Discernment is meant to serve the ultimate desire to be a living sacrifice for the glory of God. It is not merely an effort to answer the question of effectiveness, affordability, or viability. Yet in answering the question of what is most honoring given our current situation, the questions of practicality must not be seen as an absence of faith, but as the context in which we live out trust.

Through discernment, a radically personal and intuitive process joins with a radically interpersonal and prophetic path. It requires that I submit myself to spiritual reflection, including journaling, *lectio divina,* and spiritual direction. It calls me to open my heart in conversation with God and others to discern my motivation and the wisdom they offer. And then it calls for me not to assert with dictatorial certainty that God has revealed himself or that I know the will of God, but to offer humbly my understanding of what is best to do.

Decision

Individual discernment must submit itself to a community conversation with testing, refraction, and re-forming, and then the matter must be turned over to the designated decision makers for their responsible care. If implementation of the plan requires full agreement, then the result will often be a consensus-driven, watered-down plan that is designed to satisfy everyone and, therefore, pleases no one. Well before the process of communal exploration begins, the formal decision-making structure should be well articulated, put in writing, and accepted and blessed by the participants. No one should be allowed to participate who doesn't trust those who are called to make the final decision. Otherwise the labor will feel like a mockery or a ruse when a decision is made that contradicts what some stakeholders most deeply believe to be wise.

This is where a great deal of organizational politics, gossip, and harm arise. If the decision-making structure is not agreed to by everyone in advance, the people who helped form the plan often feel defrauded when the final decision is not what they desired.

Allowing sufficient time to discern how a community moves from exploration to decision making is, therefore, imperative. Whose voice predominates? Consider that word *pre*dominates. Who dominates before the process begins?

She may be the formal leader, or she may be someone who is not even in the room. It is crucial not only to know and understand the organizational chart but also to know the players whose presence is felt even when they are absent. How else will they be named and taken into account publicly at the beginning of the process? Can they be named or is the proverbial elephant in the room too big and dangerous to be acknowledged?

Truth is essential because organizations that won't tell the truth can't make good decisions. A community that hides the truth will lack character and will become a multifaceted hypocrisy. Such a community will make decisions based on the ability to hide and blame rather than on what might grow glory in both individuals and the corporate whole.

All processes committed to growing character must result in action. In meetings where discussion fails to move to dialogue or discernment, decisions will be postponed and needed action becomes futile inaction. In some instances postponement may be judicious, but it may also be a flight from the dying of deciding, from dividing and sentencing some options to death while choosing to give one possibility life.

Whether a decision is made in a committee, by a staff, with an executive team, or alone, the decision weighs on a leader. There is no way to be honest and, at the same time, wholly confident. But someone must decide and bear the mark. And as the leader, you must bear the mark publicly before your peers, subordinates, and bosses. It is for that reason you are meant to be a storyteller who tells about the character of the people in the process. The story is as much about the process and the people who wrestle well as it is about the outcome.

If the dream that most deeply motivates action and choice is the gospel, then you must publicly announce the truth of the gospel story as it weaves itself through the fibers of your story and the stories of your team members. You must do so with enormous wisdom and courage in order to invite your community to consider first its story and second how to journey more deeply into the truth that transforms your character. And you need to know this: journeying deeply will inevitably involve telling secrets and stepping into the wild water of confessing that, like everyone else, you are a limping leader.

TELLING SECRETS

The Risks of Admitting You're the Chief Sinner

I f a leader publicly discloses his failure, he has to brace himself for trouble. Such an admission troubles the self-righteous and the prodigal alike. A leader who names personal failure is saying, "There is always a way back home for anyone desperate enough to embrace what is true about the heart of man and the heart of God." Both the prodigal and the self-righteous older brother don't want to be foolish or desperate. Therefore, the honest leader who confesses he is both wayward and self-righteous disturbs the hubris of both.

The leader who admits personal failure often loses respect, risks being marginalized, and could very well be dismissed—either literally by losing his job or in practice by being excluded from the inner circle of power. Only the foolish invite honesty without being honest with themselves about its danger. To confess to yelling at your spouse, or admitting that you manipulate meetings by being intense and verbal, invites people to put you in a box and supplies them with information they could later use against you.

We are inveterate box makers because we want quick, simple categories for life. Usually we don't want a thoughtful analysis of a social issue; instead, we prefer the *USA Today* version: "Give it to me quick and clear or don't bother. I can't take the time to exercise my untapped reflective thinking to consider the depth and nuances of an issue." Also, if you give people a way to interpret you that enables them to pigeonhole your sin, you will be labeled and boxed in.

By naming some of the data of being a chief sinner, you risk losing respect that was based on false assumptions. Being honest about your failures will also marginalize your influence—if *influence* is defined as always getting your way—because you will prove false the myth that you are imbued with super-human "stuff." The honest leader who admits his chief-sinner status may be dismissed by statements such as, "He's just an angry man," "He hates conflict and is just being nice," or "You can't trust him because he said he really only wants things to go as he has planned."

Your honesty empowers those who want to control and dismiss you: they can use your own words against you. And they may because sin disappoints people and deepens their suspicion and doubt. So why would any leader divulge such information, knowing that others might misuse it? One reason is that leaders who already know they are their organization's chief sinner aren't afraid to make that truth known. Another reason is that people don't need your honest admissions to help them put you in a box. From the moment they first meet you, people are building a box for you, especially if you are perceived to have power. But the more you openly name your struggles, the less people can use your silence as a back door to blackmail you, to sabotage your leader-ship, or to subvert relationships within the organization.

Here's an example: The people at Mars Hill know that I am intense and verbal. If my forcefulness is amplified by too much caffeine, adrenaline, or irri-tation, then I can come across as angry and intimidating. I have asked those with whom I labor to help me see myself and to name when my intensity crosses the line into intimidation. Some have done exceedingly well; they have offered generous and compelling feedback. Others have used my acknowledg-ment as a hammer to smack me when they don't get their way. The result is a loss of trust and the need for me to be particularly careful when interacting with the second group—to keep the intensity low and my words few.

If you are a leader, it is not possible to be at peace with all and friends with everyone. But when you name your own failures, even if others don't name theirs, you are free to wrestle with the number one sinner rather than being caught in the web of worrying about how others see you.

Furthermore, openly acknowledging our weaknesses allows other people to join us on the healing path. A friend who is a take-hold, take-no-prisoners kind of guy told his senior staff that he needed their prayers to help him be courageous and up-front with some customers who were taking advantage of his workers. He acknowledged that he was bold at selling but often feared conflict with his customers.

His staff knew he was a great salesman but a lousy caregiver for his employees. His confession was troubling because they had never heard him admit a weakness or ask for help. My friend told me that afterward several of his key staff thanked him and admitted they had previously assumed his lack of employee care was due to his being clueless. When they heard him admit his cowardice, they both lost and gained respect for him.

Why admit your failures publicly? First, doing so invites others—by the Spirit's prompting—to look more honestly at their own need for forgiveness, freedom, and courage. It also removes the dividing wall of hierarchy and false assumptions about people in power and gives the leader who humbles himself the opportunity to be lifted up by God.[1]

HOW TO EMBRACE HONESTY

How do you embrace honesty? The answer is threefold: give up what is already painfully obvious, tell the truth without telling *all* the truth, and embrace the gospel in your failure to live the gospel.

Give Up the Obvious

Trying to hide certain things about yourself is like trying to hide your face. There are traits and patterns that people will see after being with you for only a few minutes. People tell me that I am intense. I can't see my face, but sometimes I can feel my level of excitement or irritation rising. I also know from many interactions that most people view my intensity as a liability and not a welcome gift.

When I consciously work to subdue my thoughts or ideas, those around me see that I am laboring. If I keep silent, others say that I'm withholding. If I speak, I'm often given feedback that I'm imposing. Sin is circular. It is a hopeless cul-de-sac where we always seem to get stuck. No wonder we'd rather avoid naming our struggle—our failure—over and over again.

What I can do is simply own the log in my eye. Sometimes when I'm silent, I am brooding. Sometimes when I speak after keeping silent, I am imposing. And often my intensity fails to rise to the righteousness of God. Might we confess what Paul did? He wrote, "I do not understand what I do. For what I want to do I do not do, but what I hate I do."[2]

What is most obvious to others are our most common ways of failing to love—the unique style that rises to the surface during times of shame, hurt, fear, or criticism. We tell our stories not to justify or explain away our failure but to open up conversation. Our stories will reveal both who we wish we weren't but are, as well as who we wish we were and are striving to be.

Tell Some, But Not All

There is no wisdom in telling all the truth, except in a courtroom where you must. It is not the pattern of the Bible or its leaders to tell everything that could be said. The Bible tells about David's sexual sin and his murder frankly and in significant detail, but it avoids the salacious particulars. Paul tells us he is the chief of sinners and compares himself to perverts, father- and mother-killers, and liars, and says that in comparison to them he is the worst. Yet he doesn't give us details of his sexual or relational struggles.

One of the best examples of this wise restraint is Augustine's *Confessions*, where he tells the story of his conversion. It is stark and bold. He describes his ever-present war with sexual addiction and his misuse of women. He allows us to see the contours of his struggles and, in the first several chapters of the book, moves the reader toward the confession of a great sin. As he builds to the event that is revelatory of his darkness, the writing is sensuous, alluring, titillating. Surprisingly, the event he describes is not a debasing sexual tryst but the story of his stealing a persimmon from a neighbor's tree.

Is sin trivialized by such a confession? Not at all. In fact, this is a brilliant template that helps us consider both how and what to tell. We can state in bold, thirty-thousand-foot clarity that there is within us a deep and abiding darkness that is yet to be redeemed, that cries for redemption, and that will be saved one day. It can be named lust and anger, adultery and murder. And it can be illustrated by the common, daily, almost incidental experiences in our worlds.

I need not and should not draw from my darkest and most egregious failures of love. Instead, I am to paint a picture of what is true from the data that can be found in almost any unguarded hour of my life. The data inevitably reveal why I need the gospel more than I need food, water, and air.

Embrace the Gospel

There is no way to know with utter certainty what is foolishly wise to share and what is simply stupid to offer to a particular person or group. But there are a few rules to consider. Never tell anything you haven't been given permission to offer. Every story that I relate in my books or talks has been vetted by the person or people who are part of the narrative. If I don't get permission, I sometimes alter a few dimensions of the story. But in those instances I will say, "This story is true fiction. I have changed identifying details to protect both the innocent and the guilty."

When I seek permission from my wife, children, or friends to tell a story, I ask two questions: "Is the story as I've told it accurate? And is it honoring to you?" Accuracy doesn't mean every detail has to be included, but is the story true in the sense that nothing was added that simply didn't occur and nothing was left out that would radically alter the account?

Does the true story also honor the other? A story can acknowledge that there are sinners in this world in addition to you, but is it told in a manner that honors a person's dignity? Does it show how God is inviting the other person to own up to depravity and seek forgiveness? There are struggles in my marriage that I've not publicly shared because doing so wouldn't honor my wife or me at this point in our walk in grace. The same is true in many other arenas of our lives. Will those realities one day be shared? Perhaps we will be ready at a later point, but it is also possible that we are not called to name those on behalf of our community.

The core issue is whether the matters that are shared honor the story God is inviting us to tell now. For example, every couple on earth struggles sexually. No one can escape the fact that we were once called to be "naked and know no shame." We do know shame, and our marriages are meant to redeem over a lifetime the ground that shame has scarred. But few couples are called to talk about those struggles in a public forum.

Years ago FamilyLife, a marriage ministry led by Dennis Rainey, asked if I would join with them to talk about the vows of marriage in an arena event called "I Still Do!" I did. They asked me to talk about "to have and to hold" (the calling of sexual intimacy) and to talk honestly about the realities of sexuality in a marriage with two sinners. I did. I talked tastefully and honestly about some of the damage that sexual abuse has had on my marriage. It was a risk, but it is part of the calling of my own marriage to speak about the issues that other couples are reluctant to name.

A leader must know how her character is to be lived and what stories are wise and honoring to tell. The dilemma is that there is no sure litmus test. Therefore, we will need the gospel for our failures if we are to speak wisely. We will say too little or too much. We will tell a story, and our unaddressed shame or anger will leak out and blanch the beauty of the gospel.

It is an odd business: the more I live, the more I fail. The more I fail, fall forward, and am caught by the arms of grace, the more I reveal the message of the gospel. The more I pretend to have arrived and offer others advice on how they can do the same, the more I become like the prodigal's older brother, self-righteous and angry.

THE PARADOX OF GRACE

The ironic truth that those who proclaim the gospel need it more than those who hear it is not new. It just isn't being said loudly and clearly enough in this day of spin and professionalism and big programs. These days need certain stories to be told again and again. We need to tell stories about failure and the need for grace; we need to share stories that invite the hearer to consider the wild, inverted paradox of grace. In fact, these three great paradoxes need to be told often: the already and the not yet, the call to be strong and tender, and the ways of being wise as a serpent and innocent as a dove.

Already and Not Yet

We all feel enormous pressure to be done with sin, and we simultaneously fear that we will never arrive at true maturity. We are arrogant and faithless. But Scripture invites us to live in the moment when our salvation is both fully complete and not yet finished. We live in a state of the already and not yet. Let me explain.

The Bible talks about redemption being a past-, present-, and future-tense reality. We *have been* saved. We *are being* saved. One day we *will be* saved. We commonly refer to this as "being a work in progress." No one is finished, and no one is fully redeemed, even though God calls us saints and his beloved.

Very few people actually believe that we need only the few final touches applied, yet we are greatly offended if anyone points out just how far we are from maturity. We acknowledge being sinners, but we are defensive when our sin is seen and mentioned publicly. It is natural for my self-protective heart to silence the feedback by offering either excuses or context to mitigate my failure. There were extenuating factors, we were having a bad day, or we were under too much pressure and stress. Whatever our defense, God calls us to acknowledge our failure for what it is and to deal with the log in our eye first.

It is simply true: I am still a sinner. I struggle with lust and anger or what Jesus calls adultery and murder.[3] Many people will admit they've failed, but few are willing to address the "not yet"—the still existing sins—of their lustful adultery and rage-filled murder. But leadership that tells the truth must acknowledge, "I am not yet, nor are you. Therefore, when we are together, there will inevitably be tragic failures of love."

But when we admit our failures, are we denying the Resurrection? We know we have grown, yet the distance remaining to reach the fullness of maturity and freedom in Christ is far greater than the distance we have already come. If we have any sensitivity to the length of the journey ahead, it is easy to feel overwhelmed and want to quit. It seems that so much effort goes into such little growth. Why bother? But the truth is that Jesus is alive and that our struggles actually highlight how much has been covered by God's forgiveness—rather than serving as evidence that the Resurrection is not true.

In fact, what denies the Resurrection in a leader's life is not failure but presumption. Living between the already and the not yet gives rise to the tension of living between arrogance and despair. If I don't give in to despair because I've failed—or to presumption and believe that I am better than I am—then I'm living in the tension that honors the Resurrection.

We are not living the Resurrection as real when we are either arrogant or in despair. Despair denies the power of the Resurrection. An arrogant confidence that has no room for doubt or struggle denies the fact that the Resurrection is merely the first fruits of the new harvest. The Resurrection is not the end of death. It is the beginning of the end of death; the "not yet" is still to come.

"Already and not yet" stories feast on surprise as they weave the threads of tragedy and redemption together in a brilliant blend. My children have been at the center of many of these stories. One story that I tell in my book *How Children Raise Parents* stands out. My daughter Amanda had an open bottle of alcohol in her car at a school event. She was arrested, and it began a difficult season for us all.

Amanda's home incarceration lasted ninety days. She could go to school but had to come straight home—no friends, no music, no television, no phone calls. She could do homework, read, and spend time with her mother and father. It was torture. During that time, however, she found an article in our local paper about a group of kids going to Siberia to work with orphans. She asked if she could go to the meeting, and we agreed. I knew full well she wanted a reason to get out of the house and see some friends. She had found a perfect opportunity, and I admired her resourcefulness. She came back from the meeting enthused about going to Siberia, and we agreed that she could go if she raised all the money she needed and if she continued to mature. She did both.

This trip helped shape my daughter's purpose in life. She discovered a passion for helping young women who had been—or would soon be—trafficked in the sex-trade industry. She became their passionate advocate and decided that obtaining a degree in nursing would be an effective means of engaging trafficked victims on both a physical and spiritual basis.

I was in the midst of writing the parenting book when this story was but a few months behind us. Amanda had returned home from college. She read the manuscript to assess the stories told about her, and afterward she complimented me on the manuscript. Then she asked, "Why isn't the story of my arrest and how it began to reopen my heart to God in the book?" I offered a lame excuse, and she said, "It is a painful story for me, yet I know God is written all over it. I am not ashamed of my story, Daddy. Are you?"

She was right. I still felt shame, and my choice not to tell her story was far more about covering my failures as a parent than about honoring her. The ninety days of home incarceration had required us to talk more honestly than we ever had before about our mutual failures as a father and daughter. Her redemption called me to be redeemed even as she closed her critique of the book: "I think it is a good book, but it lacks a single, overarching story that makes clear your most central premise. I think my story does that better than any other."[4] Redemption is more surprising than we can imagine.

"Already and not yet" stories don't necessarily have happy endings right away. Sometimes the stories require decades of diligent waiting before we taste the harvest. But these stories capture the imagination and remind us that one day the good work God has begun will be completed.

Strength and Tenderness

To live out the character of Jesus, we must be like God: strong and tender at the same time.[5] The conundrum is that it's easier to be just one and not the other. After all, those with strength seldom cry, and they also struggle with the need to take responsibility for their failure. On the other hand, the tender seldom risk failure or confront others about their sin. It makes sense, then, that leaders tend to be strong and not tender, and followers tend to be more tender than strong. The division of labor that results from the distribution of these qualities may appear to make life easier and more orderly, but it is a far cry from all of us living out the character of God. All of us are called to be *both* tender and strong.

But arrogance often masquerades as strength, and a concessionary pleasantness often mimics tenderness. Many leaders use bluster, bravado, and the fire and magic of the Wizard of Oz to hide their balding, paunchy frailty. Many leaders are highly verbal, and they intimidate their community with the threat of contempt. Team members and employees know well the power of a leader to publicly shame them. This awareness is enough to silence most people since the thought of responding publicly to the taunt terrifies them. Leaders often forget that public speaking is the number one fear, above even the fear of death. So the person with verbal facility and confidence to speak in public carries a totemic power to bless or curse others.

True strength, however, must be courageous enough to confess cowardice and tender enough to admit self-absorption. In addition, a limping leader must delight in the dignity of those who offer feedback about her failure even if they do so in a manner that lacks finesse or wisdom.

Wherever we see strength and tenderness in others, we must prize it and do what we can to help it grow. My children provide a nearly constant supply of stories regarding their courage (strength) and care (tenderness) for me, for my wife, and for one another. They each live with a growing level of awe and gratitude for one another.

Recently, for instance, my son and I went fly-fishing and an accident occurred where he fell and dropped his rod in fast-moving water. We both assumed it was gone for good, but we later discovered that the rod had gotten caught on a tree branch near the riverbank, at a spot that was nearly impossible to get to. When I foolishly decided to wade over to get it, I was nearly washed away by the current. It was a terrifying risk, yet we were able to retrieve the rod.

After the drama subsided, my son said to me, "Do you think a rod is worth your life?"

I sheepishly answered, "No, it was a foolish decision."

He went on to say, "What do you think it would have been like for me to lose my father over a silly rod?" His words quickened, and he said with passion, "What do you think it would have been like for me to tell my mother how her husband died? Do you understand, Dad, that I would miss you for the rest of my life?"

I was stunned. I was not only taken aback by the utter foolishness of my choice but also by the passionate and compelling voice of my son as he named my failure, set it in a larger narrative of our lives together, and then spoke to the deepest desire of my heart to matter to my son. The effect was incomprehensible: I had never felt more foolish before my son—or more loved by him.

We must tell stories like this one, stories of how we and others are being redeemed by strength and tenderness. True tenderness steps deeply and boldly into the heartache and hopes of others. It suffers, dreams, and invites a person's heart to redemption. My son called me to know that I am fiercely loved even if I am at times a fool.

Tenderness, however, can be mimicked. Two cheap imitations are pleasant concession and pallid encouragement, and neither of these offers the nourishment that human beings need. A counterfeit tenderness fails to step into the deepest heartache; it merely skims the surface of hardship rather than addressing the heart's longing for redemption. The ache for redemption in every soul calls for a strong and tender guide, and a limping leader is in a perfect position to offer such guidance. One way she does this is by telling stories.

Stories that are both strong and tender highlight the courage and kindness of the people who step into our lives to bring grace. I've told many stories in my books *Intimate Allies* and *The Intimate Mystery.* I have written about my glorious wife and her willingness to fight with strength and to surround me with tenderness to see my heart redeemed. No one has been more of a taste of God to me than my wife. At the same time I've told a number of stories about my stepping into my wife's fear and anger and loving her when the going got tough.

Those of us in ministry, especially those of us who do a lot of speaking or writing, run a huge risk of misusing our families as a ready source of endearing and redemption-oriented stories. I'd be concerned if stories about our families or ourselves were told from the pulpit on a weekly basis. Going easy on the stories—offering only occasional glimpses of the struggles in our worlds, then allowing the impact of those few stories to sift through a congregation—is a wiser approach than offering a regular fare of personal accounts that can be either overwhelming or easily dismissed as self-indulgent. With judicious use, however, the stories of how others have exposed and born the burden of our frailties powerfully reveal the wonder of the gospel.

Wise and Innocent

There may not be a more radical conundrum found in the Bible than Jesus' instruction that his followers "be as shrewd as snakes and as innocent as doves."[6] It gives me great hope that he offered that counsel as he sent the disciples on a missionary trip when they didn't know yet why he had come to earth. Like those first-century believers, we often don't know what we are doing or why we are being sent, yet Jesus sends us. And often in the going we find what we didn't know we were looking for. In this story Jesus gives his disciples an odd phrase for an odd journey, a phrase that we must assume reflects another dimension of maturity.

This instruction to be both wise and innocent is given greater impact by the similes Jesus used. To be wise like a serpent implies that we are to be no less crafty than the serpent that tempted and trapped Adam and Eve. A Christian must not be naive or foolishly innocent. We are meant to be cunning and clever as we invite others to the gospel. At the same time we are to live with the harmless presence of a dove. In the Bible a dove is a symbol of *shalom*, and at Jesus' baptism a dove signified the coming of the Spirit of God. A dove is gentle, pure, and peaceful. Our cunning must be driven by dovelike innocence. Employing cunning for the sake of redemption is not the same as using manipulation to achieve one's ambitions. You can be crafty and wise while being committed to the other person's good.

The story of Nathan confronting David with his murder and adultery gives a picture of cunning used redemptively: the prophet's clever story helped David acknowledge and repent of his sin. Solomon also illustrated this type of wisdom and innocence when he judged the two women who claimed to be the mother of the same child: his proposed solution—cut the child in half—prompted the real mother's cry: "Don't kill him!" Redemptive cunning is also found in nearly every encounter Jesus had with the political and religious authorities of his day. He asked, "Why are you trying to trap me?" and then he turned around and exposed the trap, creating a bind for them by asking them to look at a coin and answer the question, "Whose portrait is this? And whose inscription?" He then gave them an ambiguous command, "Give to Caesar what is Caesar's and to God what is God's."[7] Did Jesus answer the question? Not really, yet he exposed his enemies' desire to trap him, and he was not caught by their plot.

Yet what too often masquerades as wisdom is a spirit of know-it-all-ism, and naiveté often tries to imitate innocence. The differences in both cases are crucial. First, a legion of bright men and women know why the sky is blue and the moon sometimes has an orange tone, but they don't have to tell all they know or make others feel stupid for not knowing. But a know-it-all often uses knowledge as a weapon to impress and control others with his apparently superior acumen. Second, a naive person avoids facing the darker side of reality by looking through her rose-colored glasses. In contrast, innocence is a hunger for purity that rests in the promise of its coming day. Innocence is not fluffy optimism; it is a passionate anticipation of full redemption that purifies the heart with hope.

Telling stories of genuine innocence and wisdom calls us to admit our distorted sight. We see through a lens darkly at best, and at worst we are suspicious, doubting, and presumptive. We misread the Bible. We misread our spouses, our staff, and the convenience store clerk. We drive the opposite direction down a one-way street and think everyone else is wrong. We develop an amateur's expertise or an expert's competence, and this domain of truth we claim as ours is often the realm in which our blindness is most apparent.

Case in point. Whenever I have the chance, I love to go either fly-fishing or sailing. I have read countless books, spent time with experts, taken courses, and gained a moderate level of knowledge about both these passions. Yet as a sailor I've navigated into dangerous waters because I sailed on a true compass heading rather than by the magnetic circle. On a chart there is a compass marking with two circles: true (the outer circle) and magnetic (the inner circle). I don't recall if I was preoccupied or just not thinking, but I used the outer circle rather than the magnetic one, and by doing so, I followed a course that could have sunk our boat. Even worse, as the data began to indicate a navigational error, I refused to acknowledge the data. It was my glorious wife who kept asking obvious questions. She wasn't deterred by my irritation. She invited reflection and pressed home the contradictory data. And before disaster overcame us, I fled from the lee shore.

My wife did not ignore my failure, nor did she use it to strip me of my dignity. Instead, she offered generosity and curiosity as she stepped into my error of judgment. Her questions were cunning and kind, perseverant and wise. A bad error became a lifetime lesson, primarily because it was pursued so well by a wise and innocent woman. If we surround ourselves with wise men and women, we will have a quiver full of surprising, compelling stories to tell.

Telling the truth about ourselves—even in surprising, compelling stories— is risky but necessary. It magnifies the value of grace and invites others not to be surprised by their own desperate need of the gospel. Leaders who stumble and persevere in falling forward do so because they are caught up in the person of Jesus. In all that we do and in all that we become as leaders, we must point people to him. As we make him known to others, we introduce him as our prophet who tells the truth, our priest who comforts, and our king who serves the will of his Father. And in doing this, we find our truest calling and joy.

THREE LEADERS YOU
CAN'T DO WITHOUT

Why You Need a Prophet, a Priest, and a King

It should be clear by now: leadership is all about maturity. A leader's first calling is to grow, knowing that he is the one who has the furthest distance to mature. The more we walk the path first while becoming last and least in our organizations, the more we become like the Alpha and Omega whom we long to serve.

And what exactly does it mean to be mature like Jesus? To be like Jesus in character is to imitate his way of relating to others. We survived the "What would Jesus do?" (WWJD) craze. This is not a helpful question because what Jesus would do would be too odd for anyone to do and still keep his job. Jesus' radical and infinitely wise way of being with others enabled him to be both profoundly rude to those who needed to be disrupted and tender beyond words to those whose hearts were full of sin and shame. So if this sort of question is to be asked at all, it would be far better to ask: "How did Jesus relate to different kinds of people?" But, of course, HDJRDKP is not nearly as catchy as WWJD.

Jesus was an ambiguous, poetic parable-teller and a disruptive prophet to the self-righteous. He was a tender priest who offered the forgiveness of sin to the prostitute. And to the hungry and sick, he was a king who provided for them and protected them from harm. For centuries this multifaceted work of Christ has been referred to in terms of the offices of prophet, priest, and king. Those offices are the highest callings for service in the Old Testament. The king ran the theocracy, establishing the realm by creating an infrastructure that maintained safety, justice, and order. The realm was given meaning by the stories, art, rituals, and comfort that were the domain of the temple and the priests. And when people wandered from God's desire for them, the prophet disordered both worlds by speaking on God's behalf.

Interestingly, each of us has skills and gifts that place us primarily in one category—prophet, priest, or king. Sadly, the crisis, complexity, betrayal, loneliness, and weariness of leadership transform most prophets into troublemakers, most priests into dogmatists, and most kings into dictators. Mystery and chaos send leaders spiraling into efforts to manipulate and manage the world without drawing on faith, hope, and love. Consequently, our striving for order and meaning must be interrupted by a prophetic voice that will sing cacophony to undermine our idolatry. Prophets challenge kings to fight injustice rather than devour the poor, and they call priests to speak of hope for reconciliation instead of promising peace without requiring the necessary honesty regarding sin. Theologian François Turrettini wrote,

> The threefold misery of humanity resulting from sin (that is, ignorance, guilt, and the oppression and bondage of sin) required this threefold office. Ignorance is healed through the prophetic office, guilt through the priestly, and the oppression and bondage of sin through the kingly. The prophetic light scatters the darkness of error; the merit of the priest removes guilt and obtains reconciliation for us; the power of the king takes away the bondage of sin and death. The prophet shows God to us; the priest leads us to God; and the king joins us together with God, and glorifies us with him. The prophet illuminates the mind by the spirit of enlightenment; the priest soothes the heart and conscience by the spirit of consolation; the king subdues rebellious inclinations by the spirit of sanctification.[1]

THE THREEFOLD OFFICES OF LEADERSHIP

Turrettini reveals the great richness of the threefold office of Christ. But do these three offices encompass all aspects of leadership? Yes and no. To the degree that any schema fails to encompass all of reality, that is, all of God, it is inadequate. The one to remind us of that will be the prophet. These three categories don't address every leadership issue or role, but they do offer us rich wisdom and a helpful perspective on the life of a leader.

We are not to be solely a prophetic leader, nor priestly, or kingly. We are to be all three, all at once, and with all three in play with, for, and against one another. To lead is to mirror Jesus in all three of these capacities. But the fact is obvious: we are likely stronger in one dimension and weaker in another. And we hold the strength and weakness together by middling abilities in the third office. My strength is as a prophet. My weakness is as a king. And I am a fair-to-middling priest.

God, however, loves to use our strengths to get us into situations where our weaknesses are exposed and used for his glory. I find it hilarious that I am a seminary president. It is not what my skill set would seem to indicate. There are no occupational tests, gift inventories, personality profiles, or gut intuitions that would ever have suggested "seminary president" as a possible job for me. In exposing and using our weaknesses like this, God reminds us again and again of our dependency on him and directs our praise to the only One who is worthy of it.

God intends my life to become a reflection of all three roles as I mature. I am called to personally be a prophet, priest, and king. God also intends for those three roles to be represented in an organization by different people, and I am called to create space in our organization for all three roles.

At Mars Hill Graduate School we have a brilliant king, Ron Carucci, a seasoned and sophisticated leader who knows how to grow both people and our infrastructure. He is at the same time an exceptional prophet and a middling priest. In our mix we also have Paul, a great priest who is also gifted as prophet and king, and Ronna who is a kind queen, a tender storyteller priest, and a bold prophetess. Our leaders are breathtaking, and we need more men and women whose gifts bump up against our natural tendencies to create more chaos, therefore demanding more creativity and surrender from us all.

PROPHET, PRIEST, AND KING TOGETHER

How are these roles meant to be woven into the fabric of an organization? And what happens when a dimension of Christ's offices is lacking or is viewed as undesirable? We will look first at a secular parallel to these roles and then consider what is unique about the categories of king, priest, and prophet.

In her book *Connective Leadership,* Jean Lipman-Blumen argues that leadership involves three interactive dimensions: direct—the intrinsic, competitive, and power styles of leadership; relational—the collaborative, contributory, and vicarious styles of leadership; and instrumental—the personal, social, and entrusting styles of leadership.

The direct style of leadership takes charge and enters into the fray of competitive challenge. It calls forth excellence and uses power to move an organization through crisis and other inevitable tangles. This dimension fails when it becomes authoritarian and uses shame or fear to control the actions of others. This leadership style is successful when it continues to move toward a clear and ordered purpose. Without this leadership style, chaos will inevitably take over. This is much of the labor of a king.

The relational style of a priest, on the other hand, offers care and enters the heart with a commitment to enhance the value and significance of others. This style offers dignity, respect, and honor to those involved in an organization. The relational leader mentors and encourages personal and corporate growth through a greater focus on emotion, story, and ritual. This orientation fails when personal growth becomes self-absorbed and fails to have a goal or vision that is greater than oneself. This work is the domain of a priest.

The instrumental style of leadership influences competition and care by motivating others to new ways of seeing and acting. Lipman-Blumen writes, "[Instrumental leaders] are particularly adept at dramatic gestures and counterintuitive (unexpected or paradoxical) symbols that communicate their vision and enlist others in their cause. Their finely tuned sense of theatre, sometimes bordering on eccentricity, brings excitement, fun, and sometimes awe to their supporters."[2] This style fails when it becomes disconnected from the other two leadership styles. This is the work of a prophet who exposes, arouses, and disturbs in order to call her people back into right relationship with God.

Lipman-Blumen's categories do not fit perfectly with king, priest, and prophet, yet they overlap in some significant ways. What the biblical model of prophet, priest, and king uniquely addresses is the tension inherent among the three roles and the utter necessity for all three to engage one another for the good of the community. If we want to both magnify Jesus and become more like him, then we must make room for each dimension in our organization and strive to grow the parts of ourselves that are weak.

KING: CREATING LIFE-GIVING STRUCTURE

A king builds infrastructure to provide for the needs of his people and protect them from harm. As he works for a fair and just society, a king juggles crises, decision making, allocation of resources, talent development, and issues of survival and growth.

A king is called to be a core go-to strength in the face of uncertainty and danger, so she must be wise, vigilant, strong, and bold. When we think of leadership, this is often the primary picture that comes to mind. We look to the king to handle the crisis, minimize the complexity, and bring the anxiety of her people to a tolerable level. She imposes order on the chaos, and she does so by holding together contagious optimism and brutal honesty.

In his book *Good to Great,* Jim Collins tells the story of meeting Jim Stockdale, one of his personal heroes who had been the highest-ranking officer in the infamous Hanoi Hilton, the North Vietnamese prisoner-of-war camp. When Collins asked Stockdale how he survived, Stockdale told him that he made it because of his faith that his story would turn out well. Collins then asked what kind of people didn't survive. The former POW quickly answered, "The optimists." The optimists thought they would be released by a set date, such as Christmas, and when the date came and went, they lost their resolve to live. Collins writes,

> Another long pause, and more walking. Then he turned to me and
> said, "This is a very important lesson. You must never confuse faith
> that you will prevail in the end—which you can never afford to lose—
> with the discipline to confront the most brutal facts of your current
> reality, whatever they might be." To this day, I carry a mental image
> of Stockdale admonishing the optimists: "We're not getting out by
> Christmas; deal with it!"[3]

A king can't afford to be a pessimist, nor can he be an optimist. A king brings together honesty and hope in the midst of crisis. And he builds a team that can do the same. Jim Collins argues that people are far more important than the direction of the organization:

> The executives who ignited the transformations from good to great did
> not first figure out where to drive the bus and then get people to take
> it there. No, they first got the right people on the bus (and the wrong
> people off the bus) and then figured out where to drive it. They said,
> in essence, "Look, I don't really know where we should take this bus.
> But I know this much: If we get the right people on the bus, the right
> people in the right seats, and the wrong people off the bus, then we'll
> figure out how to take it someplace great."[4]

A king must assess talent, recognize strengths and weaknesses, and ascertain openness or capacity to change. With this data, he then determines who stays and who goes. He decides not to harbor anyone in the organization who threatens its integrity and energy. This may be where most leaders in Christian organizations fail. Most churches and nonprofit organizations have too few employees and resources to be able to endure a single piece of deadwood. The leader often fails to remove the deadwood in a timely matter, if at all.

We fail to live well as leaders if we are afraid of conflict or if we need the applause of the throngs. A king must be intimately connected to his people but also able to suffer loneliness when his decisions are not popular. He must be bold enough to make difficult decisions without being dogmatic and without adopting an arrogance that would hide his fear that his decision just might be wrong.

PRIEST: CREATING MEANINGFUL CONNECTIONS

A priest helps create meaning for the people in her organization through story. Storytelling is neither just an entertaining pastime nor just an interesting way of communicating facts or values. In *Leading Minds,* Howard Gardner writes, "The ultimate impact of the leader depends most significantly on the particular story that he or she relates or embodies, and the receptions to that story on the part of audiences (or collaborators or followers)."[5]

Gardner argues that a leader tells stories that address three core questions: What is our identity? Where are we from? Where are we going? These questions have to do with identity, both individual and corporate. A priest helps define vision and mission and, in that process, connects people to how to live (delivery of the law), how to live well (creativity), and how to live well with others (connecting symbols and rituals).

Delivery of the Law

A story is not just interesting; it actually delineates how to live. When Moses went to the people with the Ten Commandments, he went as a priest. His people were delivered from slavery through an exodus—and that is the story to be told. Stories orient us as to how to shape and order our lives. Stories offer rules that are not easy to follow even if they are clear and concise.

Stories also order chaos to some degree, and then they call us to a new depth of relating to God and to others. Priests tell stories and extrapolate principles and rules for living from that narrative. For example, priests use the Ten Commandments to reorient us to the relational implications of the story of the Exodus. A good priest establishes not only the stories to be told but also how we will relate to one another according to the core values and practices reflected in that story. A priest has to be able to articulate for his organization what values the story compels them to live.

Creativity

A priest helps the body connect to the soul through the physicality of worship, through movement and music, and by corporately creating something in an environment that is very different from home or work. By engaging a different part of the brain than logic and linearity, for example, music stirs emotion and moves us in a way logic can't. And the place of worship offers both rest and a blank canvas on which to paint something new as we engage with God and are changed by him. The priest also calls us to see and think differently as we engage our creativity, our hearts, and our bodies. The list of possibilities for bringing the body into play is endless: ropes courses, hymn fests, meeting in a cabin rather than in a boardroom, lighting candles, writing poetry, creating art.

Finally, a priest offers a context for creativity that introduces disorder, which compels new creation. The priest must lead in an engagement of the body that allows people to move through the process of order-disorder-reorder.

Connecting Symbols and Rituals

Priests brand their product, community, and story through symbols and symbolic processes. A brand is a mark, a symbol that in a condensed, poetic, intense fashion says far more than the mere sign itself. It may sound disrespectful, but sacraments are branding rituals. The cross is the ultimate brand of Christianity.

Priests use the cross and other symbols to tell the stories of faith in a more condensed and iconic fashion. University convocation and graduation ceremonies involve rituals that have been part of the academy for centuries. These rituals, similar in symbolic richness to the Lord's Supper and baptism, present the organization's core stories and truths. They connect us to those who came before us as well as those who will come after.

A priest is the master of ceremonies, the narrator who helps us find in the sermon, the sacrament, or the symbolic gesture a new lens for looking at our lives. She is both the maker of metaphor and the exegete who reads our lives in light of a symbol or metaphor. She is not merely a storyteller but a translator who brings our individual stories into the larger story of the organization.

The Kingly-Priestly Alliance

Kings and priests get along like mashed potatoes and gravy. A king sets a direction and commands his subjects to go that way. A priest offers those subjects a rationale for going on the king's campaign. The commander in chief needs a story to justify either going to war or diverting needed resources from one cause to another. The priest provides a sense of purpose for the sacrifice and brings cohesion when there could be division in the ranks.

The priest will officiate (storytell) at state functions. The priest has nothing to gain by questioning the direction set by the king, so it can easily become a chummy, mutually beneficial relationship that leads to compromise. The prophet Jeremiah exposes such false priests with this indictment:

> They dress the wound of my people
> > as though it were not serious.
> "Peace, peace," they say,
> > when there is no peace.[6]

The dishonest priest allows the stories of the faith to be used to serve the political and social agendas of the status quo. The priest gains power from the king to the degree he facilitates the demands of the king. Such an alliance enables the priest to direct his violence against the sins that need to be banished from the kingdom as he serves the king's agenda. The king can send his spies to ferret out the rule breakers and then rid the holy kingdom of malcontents. A priest often blesses such violence and overlooks the king's excesses.

At the same time the king bows to the priest's stories, acknowledging the authority of the priest to be the teller of the great myths. The king submits to the processes and procedures established by the priestly caste to keep the kingdom organized, although he may violate those rules when it's to his advantage. Often he will pay for new churches, colleges, and hospitals that are run by priests who rule religion, educate the young, and care for the sick. For the king to maintain power, society must have strong glue, and the king knows that the priests provide this.

Though priests and kings often work symbiotically, for good or for ill, there can also be great tension between them. Senior management, for instance, tends to think of the HR department as a bunch of softies who spend the day resolving the complaints of whiners. The HR department often sees senior management as cowboys and cowgirls who will ride their horses until they drop and then put them up wet. The same tensions are often apparent between a senior pastor (the king) and the executive pastor or the assistant pastors (the priests). The assistants feel they are hired to do the work the king doesn't want to do, which usually involves talking to people. The assistant sees the senior pastor as out of touch and uncaring.

At their worst, kings are bullies and priests are wimps. But as long as they give one another what is necessary for their survival, a relative peace can exist, that is, until a prophet comes to town. It is no wonder that most organizations fall into the king-priest dyad. It is also no surprise that most organizations will only occasionally allow a prophet to come into their ranks, usually in the form of a paid consultant. Seldom will an organization have the wisdom to hire and keep on staff a prophet who disrupts complacency and awakens desire through dreaming. Prophets are not the easiest people to have around.

PROPHET: CREATING COMPELLING VISION

Most people want to grow, but the price of growth is pain. A grapevine will not produce excellent wine grapes unless it is pruned. It is the way of all growth and excellence: submission to pain through discipline is the only route to maturity.

Discipline is the essential link between pain and growth. It lets the process of suffering shape us to a greater glory. Runners, for example, vary their workouts from day to day and before major runs. Otherwise the body becomes comfortable with the routine and conserves energy and reduces pain by offering only what is necessary to do the expected run. The body seems to say, "I know you. You want to run farther and faster than I'm comfortable doing, but I will make you pay if you try it. So slow down, enjoy the mileage, and there will be no pain."

Runners, therefore, employ training regimens that push them harder up hills, or they mix long runs with sprints in order to fool the body into improving without shutting down and saying, "No way." Likewise, in all of life discipline requires a breakdown of the status quo for the desired improvements to continue. Discipline reminds the body that it is the servant of the one who can imagine a faster time or a longer run.

As representative of discipline, a prophet is an odd interplay of coach, poet, visionary, and therapist. He disrupts the paradigm of comfort and complacency. But when he shouts at me, he also invites me to desire and dream of redemption. When he comforts me with the vision of what will one day be my future, he calls me to create it with a commitment to honesty, care, and justice. (If he were not a prophet but a good priest, he would tell me a bedtime story and comfort me. He might even bring me a cup of hot cocoa.) But a prophet is a far cry from a priest. This odd presence cries out, invites, and keeps telling me to move.

A prophet exposes our subtle turn to indulgence and self-congratulation. He points out our self-righteousness and underscores the evidence that our current condition is not true, good, or lovely. And often, in order to expose the unrighteousness of the current way of being, he allows himself to be a fool.

A prophet exposes what is not right in part by arousing dreams of redemption. She poetically touches ache for what is not and calls forth a vision of what will come. A prophet is more a poet than a rabble-rouser, and her poetry often contains dense metaphors and complex symbols to tap into the deepest parts of the heart. A prophet connects with the unconscious motivations, desires, and dreams that surface more through symbol than by logic. In that sense, the prophet and priest overlap. The priest moves more toward order, but the prophet uses symbol to unnerve and reveal. Both prophets and priests are poets of the soul. The priest writes and sings the psalms to open hearts to desire, whereas the prophet utters dense and complex metaphors equally to awaken hearts that have grown dull and fat.

It's no surprise, then, that the prophet-poet-disrupter is often shunned as being too weird or eccentric. To normal people, a prophet may be intriguing but unpredictable and dangerous. So often prophets are not welcome in "normal" company; instead they find solace in communities of prophets who are notorious for being self-absorbed and destructive. Those cultures can be as different as the Village in New York or a seminary in the Midwest. Prophetic communities attract artists, poets, theologians, therapists, songwriters, producers, actors/actresses, and occasionally the literal prophet. All of these have one thing in common: they want to challenge the status quo of the king and the priest.

As a result prophets are often killed or sent into exile. And it's easy to understand why. Few people want their lives disrupted by visions, poems, and stories that wreak havoc on the comforts of daily life.

The three offices of leadership—prophet, priest, and king—complement but also irritate one another. There will always be conflict and misunderstanding among the three. Members of one office will inevitably hold the other two in some degree of suspicion and contempt. But if we want to magnify Jesus and become more like him, then we must make room in our organizations for each dimension and strive to grow the parts of ourselves (individually and collectively) that are weak.

Leaders also need to make room for all three dimensions in the space of their souls. It may sound like I'm suggesting that you become a haunted and deeply divided person. But actually, we are often called to fulfill all three offices—to disrupt complacency, to bring comfort to heartache, and to direct others to life—in one sermon or a single counseling session. We must, therefore, create space in our organizations and in ourselves for this kind of rich, creative complexity.

COHERENCE WITHIN CHAOS

To the uninitiated ear, jazz sounds like a cacophony. But to the connoisseur, it sings not only with sound but also with color and texture. The rhythm of jazz may fail to offer clear order and harmony, yet over time it creates coherence without having to completely corral chaos. It forces the listener to live in the tension between order and disorder without finding resolution in the prison of regulation or the exile of anarchy.

When it comes to cacophony, nothing quite compares to the inevitable tensions between the prophet who exposes, the priest who reconciles, and the king who orders. The noise is more than most people or organizations wish to endure. Imagine, for instance, putting a tender heart (Andrew, a priest) and an impulsive troublemaker (Peter, a prophet) together with powerful leaders, such as Matthew (a tax-gatherer) and Simon (a zealot; an antigovernment revolutionary), both kings. It is a recipe for conflict. But it is God's plan to interweave chaos and order to create a mysterious music that bonds disjunctive forces into a new unity.

The king creates a strong center. The priest strengthens the center with myth and meaning. The prophet disrupts the center in order to keep it from becoming stagnant. In the disruption, a new center will be created and new meaning will be revealed. The process is unfinished until the true King comes to reign as a tender priest, to reconcile all that is broken, and to prophetically expose lies as he unveils his glorious truth.

Leadership is about making way for that day by prefiguring it in the way we both define maturity and create space for complexity to exist in our organizations. We invite that day to the degree that we give:

- kings the freedom to create infrastructure, policies, procedures, standards of performance, and compensation based on performance as well as the freedom to hire, fire, advance, and demote employees and to develop and retain talent
- priests the freedom to create mission, vision, and values that are centered on meaning, stories, and branding in order to foster connection, care, forgiveness, honor, dignity, and growth
- prophets the freedom to create new ways of thinking through encounters with truth that provoke disequilibrium, desperation, and suffering, yet lead to mystery, paradox, desire, and dreams

We must put all three types of leaders in a room and invite each of them to value the strengths of the others more than they value their own strengths. Seeing the others as more valuable and necessary can happen only to the degree that each one is a broken and limping leader.

Broken and limping leaders need one another. The king left alone will become a dictator who hates chaos. The priest on his own will fall into accommodation for the sake of avoiding conflict. A prophet alone will indulge in drama and self-absorption for the sake of escaping boredom. They need one another to elude the trap of their own narcissism. But the tension created by their interaction will inevitably be greater than the immediate benefits of that interaction. The best leaders strive to grow all three offices within themselves.

I must know my strength and natural abilities and call them good because God has blessed those traits. I must also name my greatest lack or weakness and consider why that dimension of leadership is so difficult for me. It may be biological. Very few leaders who struggle with ADD, for instance, will be inclined to be kings. For others, their struggle may be connected to personality: very few introverts will find their natural strength to be that of a priest. And there may be significant life experiences that shape our inclination as leaders: very few prophets come from well-adjusted, happy homes. Whatever the factors, God desires that we come to maturity by using our strengths to get us into significant trouble that exposes our weaknesses.

It is our weaknesses that make us most dependent on Jesus and, oddly and mysteriously, that do the most to make him known to us. I wish it weren't the case. I often pray that there might be another way, but when I most exhaust myself in the crisis and complexity of leadership by my narcissistic efforts to control and manipulate, I find that I have no one but him—and that he is more than enough:

- not enough to resolve crisis, but enough to courageously enter into it
- not enough to simplify complexity, but enough to submit to a few truths
- not enough to escape betrayal, but enough to suffer betrayal with dignity
- not enough to escape self-absorption, but enough to know comfort
- not enough to find complete healing, but enough to rest in the promise of the coming day

So we must acknowledge and embrace our weaknesses, for good can come out of them. As a broken king, for example, I paradoxically promise a new reign of righteousness. As a broken priest, I invite the heart to long for the coming day of redemption. And as a broken prophet, my fumbling proclamation of truth sets my organization on an endless journey of asking, seeking, and knocking. God redeems our brokenness.

A limping leader makes Jesus known as she clings to King Jesus to lead her, to Priest Jesus to comfort her, and to Prophet Jesus to tell her the truth. We can expect nothing more or less from ourselves and our leaders than to know Jesus better through their brokenness as well as our own. We must demand of ourselves and our leaders to limp and fall forward into the strong arms of grace:

> "My gracious favor is all you need. My power works best in your weakness." So now I am glad to boast about my weaknesses, so that the power of Christ may work through me. Since I know it is all for Christ's good, I am quite content with my weaknesses and with insults, hardships, persecutions, and calamities. For when I am weak, then I am strong.[7]

NOTES

Introduction

1. See Mark 8:35.

Chapter 1

1. For examples of Moses trying hard to talk God out of God's plan, see Exodus 3:11; 4:1, 10, 13.
2. See Jonah 2:10–3:2.
3. 1 Corinthians 1:27.

Chapter 2

1. Psalm 55:12–14.
2. See Galatians 6:9–10.
3. 2 Corinthians 1:8–9.
4. 2 Corinthians 1:5–7.

Chapter 3

1. Business Owner's Toolkit: Total Know-How for Small Business, "Intergenerational Conflict," CCH Incorporated—a Wolters Kluwer Business, www.toolkit.cch.com/text/P11_1115.asp (accessed 13 February 2006).
2. See Genesis 25:29–34 and 27:1–29.
3. See Genesis 31:33–35.
4. Genesis 32:28.
5. Genesis 32:30.

Chapter 4

1. 2 Corinthians 12:7–10.
2. 1 Timothy 1:15–16.
3. See Exodus 2:11–15.
4. For examples of Moses resisting God's call to leadership, see Exodus 3:11; 4:1, 10, 13.
5. See Isaiah 30:9–18.
6. See Exodus 18:13–27.

Chapter 5

1. The pastors and other leaders who are quoted in this book took part in a study conducted by Mars Hill Graduate School. The study was commissioned to evaluate what leaders currently face as the most significant challenges in their work—challenges that were not addressed in seminary or other training contexts. The original study involved twelve hundred pastors from traditional and emerging churches and leadership frameworks. A subsequent study was done that asked fifty random leaders from that study to interact about issues of personal challenge, frustration, failure, and maturity in the ministry. The quotes that are reproduced in this book were culled from those fifty respondents.
2. Matthew 7:3–5, NLT.
3. G. K. Chesterton, *Orthodoxy* (San Francisco: Ignatius, 1995), 93.
4. Philippians 1:21–26.
5. I was present at the lecture to hear her make this statement.

Chapter 6

1. 1 Corinthians 1:18–19, 27–30.

Chapter 7

The epigraph for this chapter is Ecclesiastes 4:1–4.

1. Michael Maccoby, *The Productive Narcissist: The Promise and Peril of Visionary Leadership* (New York: Broadway, 2003), 9.

2. Jonah 4:1–4.

3. Jonah 4:5–10.

Chapter 8

1. 1 Timothy 3:5.

2. Middle English *trouthe, trothe,* variant of *treuthe,* from Old English *treowth, truth.*

3. See Galatians 6:2.

4. See Romans 12:15.

5. My editor wrote the following words after he read this chapter. "Dan: This chapter eloquently describes the plight of the lonely leader and compellingly sets forth the causes. The one need that is not fully answered is this: How does a lonely leader find a friend who will enter into the troth of a type that is described here? Is it trial and error? The leader risks vulnerability and is rebuffed by person A, so the leader approaches person B hoping for a more favorable outcome? And if person B rebuffs the leader, then he or she plows ahead with transparency and vulnerability with person C? And so forth until the leader finally finds the one person who will enter into the troth of weeping and rejoicing?"

In response, I wrote: "Ron: I don't know. Friendships continue to be one of the hardest and most painful aspects of being a leader. I have many friendships that have grown and thrived for thirty to forty years. On the other hand, during the years of living at Mars Hill Graduate School, I have lost many dear friends who, over time, have come to call me everything from liar, betrayer, manipulator, and narcissist, to dog and thief. One in particular I went to five times asking what was happening between us and what was causing our divide. He said, 'Nothing. You are imagining something that is not true.' After he departed he told many people that I was not a man who would or could receive feedback. Sadly, there was and is truth to his remark. When I shared his words with my wife, she offered a number of reasons why I am quite difficult to confront. But there have been prayers, searching, and humbling work happening in that area.

"The slide is currently occurring in another relationship. Efforts to address it are fruitless, and I can hear the remarks coming again: 'You are too difficult to love and too unwilling to change.' The temptation is raw to quit or to hide. But the risk of going to person B, then C, as you mention, and then going through the alphabet to start on AA draws me to the narrative of Jesus going to his friends three times just to ask that they might stay awake and pray. They didn't. But he continued going back. Such was his desperation. May I remain desperately longing for friendships with any who truly desire to know and serve truth and who claim to be open to troth as the path for knowing, let alone living, the truth."

Chapter 9

1. My editor asked me the following questions after he read chapter 9. "This chapter convincingly exposes the lie of busyness, but it does not offer a solution to a related conundrum. How can a leader convince her elder board or board of directors to support her in the pursuit of the paradox of limping leadership; that is, serving Jesus and not expedience or productivity? As much as a leader might want to set off on the Jesus-oriented path, she also wants to not lose her job. Can you show leaders how to bring along their board so that Jesus can be served and the leader can also keep her job?"

My response ran along these lines: "Ron: Leave me alone.

"The issue you raise is unaddressed because doing so would be inviting many leaders to risk being fired. And being fired for reading and pondering this book would not be good for sales, would it?

"The application of this truth lies somewhere between admitting that your hectic life is morally bankrupt and growing in wisdom as to how you communicate that to a boss, staff, or church that may wish for a balanced life for its people but can't do so for fear of the applecart being tumbled.

"Institutions are not idolatrous or, for that matter, even sinful; people are. Yet the systems that create norms or demand certain kinds of values—ones that are partially biblical but not built on the radical demands of an inverted, limping style of leadership—are hard to pin down. Systems often need to be exposed as much as, if not more than, the sin of the individuals who sustain them. Consequently, the risk of challenging systemic and often unstated norms may result in having the tanks roll over you to quell the rebellion.

"I wish there were another way to expose the lie of busyness. The only warrant to do so is seeing it as both honorable and inevitable as we read the story that God is wanting us to write as leaders."

Chapter 10
1. Fyodor Dostoevsky, *The Brothers Karamazov* (New York: Knopf, 1992), 257.

Chapter 11
1. See 1 Corinthians 10:31.
2. 1 Timothy 1:15–16.

Chapter 12
1. Hebrews 3:13.
2. I have heard Dick Averbeck make this statement and pose these questions both in personal conversation and in lectures.
3. A topic such as discernment can't be covered well in the space available. Discernment is a matter of such importance and is so seldom addressed that I strongly encourage you to be aware of the

work of Ruth Haley Barton at the Transforming Center (www.thetransformingcenter.org); also her work on discernment: *Invitation to Solitude and Silence: Experiencing God's Transforming Presence* (Downers Grove, IL: InterVarsity, 2004).

Chapter 13

1. See James 4:10.
2. Romans 7:15.
3. See Matthew 5:21–28.
4. For more on Amanda's story and other parenting-related tales of "the already and the not yet," see Dan B. Allender, PhD, *How Children Raise Parents: The Art of Listening to Your Family* (Colorado Springs, CO: WaterBrook, 2003).
5. See Psalm 62:11–12.
6. Matthew 10:16.
7. Mark 12:17.

Chapter 14

1. François Turrettini, quoted in Alister E. McGrath, ed., *The Christian Theology Reader* (Oxford: Blackwell, 2001), 283.
2. Jean Lipman-Blumen, *Connective Leadership: Managing in a Changing World* (New York: Oxford University Press, 2000), 124.
3. Jim Collins, *Good to Great: Why Some Companies Make the Leap…and Others Don't* (New York: HarperCollins, 2001), 85.
4. Collins, *Good to Great*, 41.
5. Howard Gardner with the collaboration of Emma Laskin, *Leading Minds: An Anatomy of Leadership* (New York: HarperCollins, 1996), 14.
6. Jeremiah 6:14.
7. 2 Corinthians 12: 9–10, NLT.

Where has your leadership journey taken you? Up the corporate ladder? Into the wilderness? On a lonely vigil? Into your deepest self? To your knees?

the LEADERSHIP CRUCIBLE

Journey with us to a different place.
Experience leadership in a whole new way.
MHGSCONFERENCES.COM

God wants to reveal Himself through your story.

As you understand what God has written into your past, He will show you how to follow Him into the future.